a star reborn

Great Southern Hotel KILLARNEY

a star reborn

Great Southern Hotel KILLARNEY

1854 - 2004

British Library cataloguing in Publication Data
A CIP catalogue record for this book
is available from the British Library

Edited by Elizabeth MacAulay
Designed by Conleth Adamson - Artworks
Printed and bound by ColourBooks

ISBN 1-899047-97-2

First published in 2003 by
Great Southern Hotels Group Limited
6 Charlemont Terrace,
Crofton Road,
Dún Laoghaire,
Co. Dublin

Distributed to the book trade by
A. & A. Farmar
Beech House
78 Ranelagh Village
Dublin 6
Ireland
Tel: +353 1 496 3625
Fax: + 353 1 497 0107
Email: afarmar@iol.ie
Web: farmarbooks.com

contents

foreword

In 2004, the Great Southern Hotel in Killarney celebrates 150 years of hospitality. During that time it has brought great joy and happiness to thousands of guests. But it has endured troubled times too. Economic recessions, political instability, war; all sound like modern day influences, but they are not. And the Great Southern survived through them all.

It did more than survive, it prospered, and the major restoration of the property, which my Board undertook in 2002, sets up the hotel for another century of success.

But the Great Southern is more than just a hotel. It is the heart of Killarney tourism, it is an Irish legend, and it has been and remains the home of a wonderful tradition of hospitality, epitomized by the professionalism and warmth of its staff.

To celebrate the 150 years the Board requested Frank Corr to chronicle the history of the hotel, to capture its soul, to immortalise its characters, and to wish her fair wind as this legend sets forth on a voyage to the 22nd century.

I hope you enjoy the read as much as I have.

Noel Hanlon
Chairman
Great Southern Hotels

words of thanks

A book such as this is a collaboration between many people and I am eternally grateful to those who freely gave of their knowledge, resources and time to the project.

Particularly valuable were the memories and wisdom of Paddy MacMonagle, Frank Lewis, Finbarr Slattery, Joe Buckley and Judge Dermot Kinlen, each of whom has a keen sense of history and specialist knowledge about Killarney and its Great Southern Hotel.

The Trustees, Management and Staff of Muckross House were most generous in opening their archives and guiding me to valuable source documents as were the librarians at Killarney and Tralee public libraries.

My thanks also to Paddy O'Brien and Marcella Doyle of the Irish Railway Archive at Córas Iompar Éireann, Heuston Station, for their help in tracking down elusive information hidden among the records of Ireland's Railway Companies.

Deirdre Parkinson, architect at Traynor O'Toole, has a wonderful sense of the hotel and its history as does fellow architect Garry Miley, and a visit to the Irish Architectural Archive yielded fascinating details thanks to the help and courtesy of its staff.

For first-hand knowledge, memories and impressions of the 'Great Southern', I needed to travel no further than the hotel itself and listen to the scores of anecdotes and off-beat facts provided by present and former managers and staff members including the general manager Conor Heneghan, former general managers Michael Rosney and the late Brendan Maher, P. J. Hartnett, Paddy Ryan, Jackie O'Sullivan, Mossie Horgan, Tommy Regan, Richard Whelan and Teresa Keogh. Their memories are enshrined in this story.

Elizabeth MacAulay was her usual patient and professional self as copy editor and the book was given its distinctive style by graphic designers Conleth Adamson and Tony O'Reilly at Artworks, who worked closely with John Harold and his team at ColourBooks.

A very special thanks to my wife, Irene, who allowed me to plunder family time during the research and writing.

And finally a special word of thanks to Eamon McKeon, chief executive of Great Southern Hotels, who initiated the project and allowed me the freedom to write the story as I found it.

Frank Corr
January 2003

Chapter 1

CHAPTER 1

A Mystic Mist

From the very dawn of history the stunning beauty of Killarney has enchanted all who have lingered among its mountains, lakes and valleys.

A young shepherd at dawn watching the first light of day pierce the mist along the Black Valley.

A sentry with shield and sword guarding the Gap of Dunloe.

A monk meditating at sunset on the hill of Aghadoe.

A merchant climbing slowly on horseback towards Molls Gap.

From earliest pre-history, since the mythical days of the Fir Bolgs and Tuatha de Danaan, Killarney has been a special place, spiritual, economic and strategic. Generation after generation left signs and relics of its importance, although it was a long, long time before they left evidence of appreciating its spectacular beauty.

For more than a thousand years this part of the Kingdom of Kerry was the domain of Irish chieftains like the great O'Donoghue, who, according to legend, lives beneath the Lower Lake and can sometimes be seen riding on its waters. Warlike, scholarly and, above all, hospitable, these ancient descendants of the Celts welcomed the first visitors to Killarney, feasting in their fortresses on Kerry mutton and mead, to the sound of the harp.

Mingling with the second wave of Norman invaders, they became the 'Old Irish', with chieftains like Donal Mor Mac Carthy, Earl of Clancar, enjoying a high level of independence from the Crown, until English rule finally asserted itself throughout Munster and, after Cromwell, vast tracts of land around Killarney were granted to military families like the Brownes, the Earls of Kenmare.

When Queen Elizabeth 1st appointed Sir Valentine Browne as Surveyor General in Ireland in 1559, she was rewarding a loyal servant for many a good deed. He used his new position to 'acquire' land confiscated from Irish families involved in the ill-fated Second Desmond Rebellion in 1583. He added to his estates by picking up, for a pittance, large tracts of land mortgaged by MacCarthy Mor, including Ross Castle and land around the Lakes of Killarney. A series of well-planned marriages into local land-owning families enhanced the riches of the Brownes. The Catholic family managed to keep its lands intact through the Cromwelliam period and subsequent support for James 2nd resulted in the monarch conferring the title Viscount Kenmare on Sir Valentine Browne in 1689. The defeat of James at the Battle of the Boyne resulted in the Brownes temporarily losing much of their lands, but by 1726 they had regained possession of what had become a run-down estate. The Third Earl, also called Valentine Browne, set about restoring its fortunes and achieved his goal in less than a decade.

It was these English families who were to create not only the town of Killarney, but also the world-famous tourist destination that exists today.

The Gap of Dunloe, Killarney *(Lawrence Collection, National Library of Ireland)*

Certainly the town did not exist in 1656 when the Down Survey was published, nor a few years later when Sir William Petty compiled a Barony map, neither of which mention Killarney. Another ninety years was to elapse before the fourth Lord Kenmare, an energetic young man, came of age and inherited the vast estates. He set about building roads through the (and his) Kingdom, linking Kenmare, Dingle and Tralee with each other and with Cork and Limerick. This was a most expensive undertaking, but it paid off in terms of stimulating trade, collecting tolls and making it easier to move troops and rent collectors.

Young Lord Kenmare also set about building a new town close to the family home, which he called Cill Áirne. It was originally just a few streets of houses for workers at the local mines and linen mills, but, like all settlements, it tended to grow and within a century had a population of around 5,000.

Towns, however new, generate commerce, and commerce generates visitors. They began to arrive in Killarney - merchants, visiting justices, soldiers, buyers of sheep and cattle, and they needed accommodation. Some attempt seems to have been made to provide for this need but early efforts at inn keeping were rather poor. Arthur Young, a writer and agriculturalist who visited the 'new town' of Killarney in 1778, reported that the general standard of accommodation was 'miserable' and 'the lodgings little better'. He added that 'visitors stay only as long as they need to'.

John Carr, another English travel writer, who visited Killarney 38 years later in 1800, found that facilities had indeed improved. He compared Killarney to Newport on the Isle of Wight, reporting that 'its streets are crowded with people - it is the principal town in the county of Kerry'.

Arriving late in the evening, he found 'a very respectable hotel, so crowded that I could scarcely make my way to the landlord, to learn that he had not even a vacant chair in his house. I drove, by his recommendation, to an inn kept by a Mrs Murphy, which I found to be more quiet and very comfortable.'

After a 'late dinner', John Carr decided to explore the area around the town. 'The lustre of a new moon, occasionally obscured by light clouds, induced me to walk to Ross Castle, about two miles distant, to the shores of the lower lake. As I stood by this hoary pile, the stupendous mountains and dusky islands finely reflected in the water, which resembled a dark mirror, the soft brightness of the lunar light, the sound of distant cascades, and a boat moving, as if by magic to the shore, formed a sublime and solemn scene, too powerful and impressive for the pen to convey.'

On the following day John Carr visited 'Mucruss', the estate of H.A. Herbert Esq. He describes how 'the richest scenery opened upon us: the ground gently undulating, clothed with vivid green verdure, the effect of the great humidity of the climate here, was adorned with almost every variety of shrubs, flourishing in the highest beauty and perfection. The graceful ruins of Mucruss Abbey, half embossed in a group of luxuriant and stately trees, influenced, as soon as seen, the bridle of our horses.'

Gradually a trickle of visitors, principally writers, were drawn to Killarney and the townspeople responded by making the place more presentable. Isaac Weld who visited in 1812, six years after John Carr, found 'three good inns' and recorded that Killarney was 'the neatest of small towns in Ireland'.

The three 'inns' described by Mr Weld in 1812 seem to have become 'three hotels' by 1820 when G. M. Smith became the first guide book writer to list Killarney and its facilities.

These first 'tourist reports' on Killarney were of little influence as the books and guides had small readerships and in any event there was little incentive for their largely English subscribers to visit Ireland, not alone make the arduous journey to Kerry.

Of somewhat greater influence were the novelists, poets and 'intellectuals' who began to arrive from 1820 onwards, when English society was wallowing in a 'romantic' period. The first arrival was Sir Walter Scott, who by then enjoyed a reputation as a literary giant in England with his novels *Ivanhoe, Rob Roy* and poems like *Lady of the Lake*. Scott had a keen interest in Ireland and was a great admirer of Dean Swift, even publishing an edition of the cleric's waspish works.

In 1809, Scott wrote to an actress friend variously known as 'Miss Smith' and 'Mrs Bartley', that he had 'heard much of the wonders of Killarney, that I hope I shall one day pay them a visit.'

The opportunity did not arise for 14 years until 1825 when Scott undertook a tour of Ireland. The tour took him from Dublin through Wicklow and westward to Limerick and Kerry. Having 'slept miserably' in Listowel, the party had breakfast in Tralee which, Scott reports, had superseded Killarney as the principal town of Kerry. Travelling onwards to Killarney they visited Muckross Abbey, went boating on the lakes, had a picnic on one of

Muckross Abbey *(Lawrence Collection, National Library of Ireland)*

the islands and admired the mountains, which Scott wrote 'are very fine, but they are exactly of the same character with the Highlands, without being comparable either for beauty or grandeur, to the best of that region.'

Scott and his party which included the novelist, Maria Edgeworth, also encountered a grisly aspect of what awaited the early 19th. century visitor to Muckross Abbey.

'The Abbey is small and without ornamental architecture, but the most perfect, and I think, by far the most impressive specimen I have ever seen. It is absolutely clothed with ivy, and mantled with giant trees, and being the holiest burying ground in Ireland among the Papists, there is an air of mortality and misery heaped upon the original wildness and gloom of the place, the like of which I had never imagined. The resort for burial is so great that they decompose the bodies by means of lime, and then after but a year or two, take out the bones and pile them up to make room within the small vaults for more Tybalts green in earth. The whole

Lower Lake, Killarney *(Lawrence Collection, National Library of Ireland)*

place is strewn with skulls and bones and some Cockneys have written Hamlet's address to Yorick's head piece on half a dozen of them.'

John Carr had also come across this scene during his visit in 1806. He was told that according to tradition, many Irish kings and chiefs are buried at Muckross Abbey, 'where the dead are buried only on the south and east sides - the north is looked upon, I was told, as the Devil's side and the west is preserved for unbaptised children, for soldiers and strangers.'

He noticed that some of the windows of the Abbey were larger than others and enquired from his guide why this was so.

'By my shoul', replied the guide, 'the great windows were for the fat friars to look through and the smaller ones for the little friars.'

Things don't change.

Despite good weather, island picnics and boating trips, Sir Walter Scott left Killarney unimpressed. 'On the whole, Killarney disappointed us all', he wrote.

Not that the townspeople did not do their best to impress their distinguished visitor. The *Cork Mercantile Chronicle* reported on 8th August 1825 that 'On Thursday, Sir Walter Scott, Bart, arrived at the Kenmare Arms Hotel, where due preparations had been made, and his arrival expected for the last few days...Strangers were pouring in fast, with a view of witnessing such an assemblage of genius and talent.'

The party was even invited to a local wake, but declined, resulting in the widow later telling friends 'that she was the more in distress as the circumstances prevented her having the honour of seeing Miss Edgeworth and Sir Walter Scott'.

Nor was this literary visit quickly forgotten. Some 22 years later, in 1849, a boatman told a visiting journalist that he 'gloried in having rowed Sir Walter Scott and Miss Edgeworth', which he added, 'was a compensation to him for having missed a hanging which took place that very day.'

A more fanciful visitor to Killarney was Lady Chatterton who published her *Rambles in Ireland* in 1830. It was well named, for her account of a tour through the country was indeed rambling and romantic. She arrived in Killarney on a Tuesday in 1828 and immediately declared that 'it is impossible to write here - beautiful visions crowd on the mind too rapidly for the hand to record. It is a region of enchantment - a hundred descriptions of it have been made, but no description that I have read, or sketch that I have seen, made me familiar with Killarney. The Upper Lake, the Lower Lake, Muckruss and Innisfallen, must be seen to be understood. It is the colouring, the gleam of sunshine, the cloud, the tone, the effect - what in short cannot be conveyed by the pen without the cant of art, and is beyond the power of the pencil, that gives a magic to the scenery of Killarney', she wrote in a style later to be developed by estate agents.

And the good Lady C was not finished. She went on:

'I say, beyond the power of the pencil, because everything changes its hue so rapidly, and the forms of objects seem to change with their colour, it is impossible to convey the variety of images presented to the eye; the eye may follow them, as it follows the flash of lightning, but to record faithfully, requires thought and profound repose, which dwell not here. The aspect of nature is ever varying from grave to gay.....Oh Killarney, thou art the most delightful, provoking place that I ever visited, and therefore I am determined not to write one more word about thee.'

Would that she meant it.

Instead, Lady Chatterton, who was indeed well named, rambles on with tales of the Chieftain O'Donoghue rising from the Lakes of Killarney on May mornings.

'I think', she concludes, 'there can be little if any doubt that the Chieftain, around whom with the first young glance of spring, spirits from all the lakes deep bowers, glide over the blue wave, scattering flowers, was a beloved leader of the Irish, who among his mountain fastnesses in Kerry, perished, heading the few and faint, but fearless still, that opposed the victorious troops of the English Parliament under the command of Ludlow.'

And with that convoluted sentence, she turns her attentions to Kildare.

More sober in life and writing style were Mr and Mrs S.C.Hall who visited Killarney regularly between 1840 and 1865 and who wrote about the town in their Guide Books which were published annually. An early edition records that Killarney had a capacity for sleeping 500 visitors and that every child was trained to be a guide. But more of the Halls later.

Just one mention however of that not so amiable curmudgeon, William Makepeace Thackeray, who wrote his *Irish Sketchbook* in 1842 and who had little positive to say about any place he visited - from the Shelbourne Hotel in Dublin to the Roundwood Inn in Wicklow. His memories of Killarney are of 'miserable conditions, people dressed in rags and living in the gut d he had no time at all for the glory of the landscape, the fine houses of the Kenmares and Herberts or the romanticism of 'Heaven's Reflex', all of which was par for his particular course.

Not that his sullen criticism had much impact even among his readers in England. The word had spread that Killarney just had to be seen, and events were about to take place, which would make that dream possible.

Chapter 2

CHAPTER 2

The Road To Heaven

The Road to Heaven may not be paved with gold, nor indeed is the Road to Heaven's Reflex.

Yet the tarmac roads and continuously welded rail on which visitors travel to Killarney today would appear to be 'miraculous' to the intrepid adventurers who journeyed to The Kingdom up to the beginning of the 19th Century.

Until then the only means of public transport was the Mail Coach, a carriage capable of accommodating up to six people inside its compartment with a further two sitting in the open air alongside the driver. The Mail Coaches were drawn by two or four horses which had to be rested or changed about every 20 miles, usually at Coaching Inns which existed since the 17th century. Many journeys took 24 hours or longer and Mail Coach passengers and driver would frequently stay overnight at an Inn before continuing their journey on the following morning.

The roads over which these coaches travelled were no better than dirt tracks in many parts, the exceptions being stretches built by local landlords who collected tolls from passing traffic. Indeed it was not until the early 1800s that professional road building began to emerge, initially around Dublin and later in the provinces, an outstanding example being the road linking Kenmare with Killarney, built around 1830 and designed by Alexander Nimmo.

Even then the traveller who wanted to visit Killarney faced a formidable challenge and a journey of considerable discomfort. If the visitor was English, the initial part of the journey involved travelling by stage coach to a port in Wales and embarking on a sailing ship which could take anything from a few days to a few weeks to cross the Irish Sea. When eventually the ship reached Dublin Bay, it would sail up the Liffey as far as Capel Street, beyond which point the river was no longer navigable. It was here that passengers disembarked and here too that some of Dublin's first hotels were established by traders of English extraction.

These first Dublin hotels were places of rest, sleep and perhaps recuperation, rather than bustling centres of social activity. That role was filled largely by a number of semi-private clubs and public coffee houses, grouped around the Royal Exchange (now Dublin City Hall) and extending into Temple Bar. This was a thriving and prosperous place in the final decades of the 18th century, its wide streets filled with the shops of silk and wool merchants, clockmakers, silversmiths, printers, stationers and the many services which were in demand by the population of a then booming city.

The traveller arriving from England would meet up here with Dubliners who shared the common goal of reaching Killarney. By the late 18th century, a network of Coach Routes radiating from Dublin had been established. Coaches departed for the Provinces on Tuesdays, Thursdays and Saturdays, returning to the capital on the intervening days.

Coach operators and hoteliers were quick to appreciate the mutual benefits of having coaches depart from and arrive at particular hostelries, a tradition continued in later years by buses. As early as 1788, a group of Dublin hotels had signed up as departure points for coaches. Hynes Hotel in Tighe Street was the terminus for

The Gardens at the Railway Hotel, Killarney *(Lawrence Collection, National Library of Ireland)*

the coach to Athlone, Drumsna and Galway while Sandy's Hotel in Smithfield was the starting point for passengers travelling to Leitrim.

The most renowned of Dublin's coaching hotels was the Royal Hibernian on Dawson Street and it was here that travellers to Killarney would congregate. While other hotels were the terminus for a single route, the Royal Hibernian was something of a 'Coach Arus' or Central Station and the departure point for coaches to Ballinasloe, Galway, Birr, Limerick, Sligo and Tullamore.

No direct service to Killarney existed, so travellers would have to take the coach to Limerick where they would pick up a connecting service at Cruises Hotel. Alternatively they could board the coach to Cork which operated from nearby Mackens Hotel. This service departed promptly at 6pm each evening and reached Cork by 4pm on the following day.

CHAPTER 2

The Mail Coaches were a familiar and colourful sight throughout the country up to the middle of the 19th century as they dashed along the roads, their coachmen blowing horns to warn the keepers of turnpikes and toll roads to open their gates. Inside and on top, the passengers bumped and swayed as the badly sprung wheels negotiated ruts, pot holes and streams, until at last a staging post was reached and driver, horses and passengers could recover sufficiently to face the next stage of their journey.

Despite these hazards, a growing number of travellers did visit Killarney during the early 19th century. By 1828, Crofton Croker was able to report that there were two hotels in the town - Gerhams Hibernian Hotel in High Street and the Kenmare Arms in New Street.

The road journey to Killarney became a lot more pleasant after 1820, thanks to the remarkable Charles Bianconi, who almost single-handedly revolutionised public transport in Ireland. He was born in Italy in 1786 and came to Ireland in 1802 at the age of sixteen. From a very early age the young man had all the talents of an entrepreneur and within months of arriving at Clonmel, he had set himself up in business, selling paintings and prints to the public. The area of operation soon expanded into neighbouring towns and counties, but the efficiency he demanded in getting his goods to market was severely hampered by the inefficiency of the local coaches. So young Charles decided to provide his own transport and to offer an improved service to the public. It was in 1815 that the first Bianconi car linked the towns of Clonmel and Cahir. The service was a tremendous success and within months the Italian teenager had quit the business of selling paintings and immersed himself totally in the business of transportation. His horse-drawn cars were light, well sprung, painted a bright red and yellow, and were pulled by up to six horses. They tended to cover short journeys linking towns and by using the network it was soon possible to travel to many parts of the country. By 1825 the service linked Cork, Limerick, Portumna, Dungarvan, Kilkenny and Wexford.

Charles Bianconi formed a lifelong friendship with Daniel Hearne, a Clonmel hotelier and he developed strong business relationships with hoteliers throughout the country. He chose the staging posts for his coaches with great care. The hotels had to provide adequate stabling for the horses, a farrier, stablemen, food and a comfortable lounge for passengers. In return he guaranteed a daily supply of customers and an element of prestige.

By 1832 the 'Bians', as the coaches were known, were covering 1,632 miles a day, servicing more than 30 towns, including Killarney.

Known as 'King of the Roads', Charles Bianconi had become a wealthy man, a close friend and ally of Daniel O'Connell and a supporter of Father Matthew, the 'Apostle of Temperance' and Edmund Rice, founder of the Christian Brothers.

But his fame was short-lived.

While Bianconi made an enormous contribution to the development of public transport in Ireland, the death knell of horse-drawn coaches was sounded with the arrival of the Age of Steam. The harnessing of the energy generated when water is heated to boiling point, revolutionised Western society in the early 19th century. It facilitated the development of powerful machinery which could perform the work of hundreds of manual labourers and was the technological driving force behind the Industrial Revolution. Steam created millions of jobs in new industries, the first industrial millionaires and whole generations whose standard of living (if not quality of life) was raised by the wealth-creating force of the steam engine.

Late 19th century horse-drawn cars

In no field of activity did steam have a greater impact than in transportation. Steam engines powered ocean-going liners and the new railways which were linking cities throughout much of the developed world.

Ireland entered the steam age in 1834 with the opening of a railway line linking Dublin with Kingstown (Dún Laoghaire).

The Dublin-Kingstown line was the first of a network of railways which would soon link the principal population centres of Ireland, transporting people and goods to every corner of the island, more quickly, more efficiently, in greater comfort and at less cost than could be imagined a few decades previously. The Iron Horse was destined to replace the fine prancing animals of the coaching era and it was only a matter of time before the Bianconi coaches would become curiosities of a bygone age.

Predictably the development of the railways was opposed by vested interests whose businesses were threatened by the new system. When plans were announced to extend the rail lines to Cork and Belfast with branches to Kilkenny, Limerick, Waterford, Navan and Enniskillen, protest meetings were organised by operators of coaches and canal boats. Charles Bianconi was a prominent figure at such meetings but he was not there to oppose progress. Indeed he was a champion of the railways and became a shareholder in several of the companies which had been set up to develop branches of the network.

Nor did his car service collapse immediately. In 1843, nine years after the opening of the Dublin-Dún Laoghaire line, Bianconi still had 100 coaches and 1,300 horses on the road, servicing areas like Donegal which had yet to be reached by the rail lines and providing a 'feeder service' to the principal railway stations.

Inevitably however, the railways took over and Charles Bianconi wound down one of the great enterprises in Irish business history and one which played a key role in the development of the hotel industry in Killarney and throughout much of Ireland.

Train frenzy had then gripped the country. Everyone, it seemed, wanted to enjoy the heady excitement of hurtling through the countryside, viewing the landscape and experiencing new places. Bianconi, it is true,

The Royal Hibernian Hotel, Dublin, starting point for stage coaches 'Hotel and Catering Review'

had opened up the roads of Ireland and made it possible for people to travel long distances, in reasonable comfort, at a price which a sizeable minority of the population could afford. But trains were a different prospect altogether, for they could carry hundreds of passengers on a single journey, accommodate them in carriages which were insulated from the weather, and get them to their destination, over smooth rail tracks, at a speed never contemplated until then. Never had there been such a revolution in transport and Ireland would not see anything similar until the arrival of commercial aircraft in the 1930s.

The Dublin-Kingstown Railway was something of a sensation in the city, providing virtually all citizens with a chance to travel along the coast to the lovely Victorian resort. It was ahead of developments in Britain and proved to be a tourist attraction, with Londoners making the long journey to Dublin, just to take the train ride.

Its success was recognised by Irish entrepreneurs and financiers and before long, everyone with money, it seemed, wanted to invest in the railways. Up to 30 companies were formed to develop railway lines and they found ready investors and support from bankers. Not all succeeded of course and many an Irish family lost its savings through investments in failed railway enterprises.

By far the most successful of the new rail developers was the Great Southern and Western Railway Company which opened its first line linking Dublin with Carlow in 1846 and later extended its interests with a line to Wicklow and Wexford. The company was also the chief motivator in developing various new railways into a cohesive network. William Dargan, a Carlowman, was the driving force in co-ordinating the plans of the railway companies and is remembered as the 'Father of the Irish Railways', while architects like John Skelton Mulvany designed a series of imposing termini which are fine examples of the confidence of the Victorian era, and include the stations at Kingsbridge and Amiens Street in Dublin which have recently been modernised without losing their original character.

The entrepreneurs who invested in the first Irish railways were people of remarkable vision, who from an early age realised that they could make profit not only from transporting passengers between towns and cities, but also by accommodating and feeding them on arrival. And so the concept of the Great Irish Railway Hotel was born.

The first railways were relatively short, linking Dublin with places like Kingstown and Wicklow, but as their success became apparent, so did the vision of the railway companies grow and the network began to develop at great speed. As with any speculative enterprise, railway investors initially looked at projects which would have maximum income and minimum risk, and so they built lines from Dublin to large population centres such as Belfast, Cork and Limerick. A town like Killarney was not a high priority because of its small population and an uninviting market for business travel or the transport of goods.

Lord Kenmare had other ideas, however. He had been aware of the potential of making money from visitors for some time and had begun to issue tickets which allowed holders to tour his lands surrounding the Lakes of Killarney or to walk to the Torc waterfall and other scenic parts of his demesne. As the principal architect of the town of Killarney, and its most significant landlord, he also had a strong vested interest in the economic development of the area. Lord Kenmare therefore set about convincing the Great Southern and Western Railway Company to extend the rail network to Killarney. Initially he received a cool reaction as the directors were not very interested in extending the line beyond Limerick, although they had a plan to go as far as Tralee, which was the principal business town in Kerry.

The Killarney group was determined to stake its claim in the new steam era and as early as 1846 it had established the Killarney Junction Railway Company, with the stated objective of bringing the rails to their town.

This company stimulated the enthusiasm of the Great Southern and Western directors. They agreed to invest in the Killarney Junction Railway Company and to co-operate with it in building a line from Mallow to Killarney. The estimated cost of the 41 miles of railway was £375,000 of which £100,000 was provided by the GS and WR. The contract for building the line was given to William Dargan. It was a massive undertaking, with 300 men employed day and night on the Bower Cutting alone and more than 1,000 men may have been employed at various stages of the work at a wage of about six pence (2c) per day. In December 1853 the *Kerry Evening Post* reported that 'the working people of Millstreet and Killarney are now well fed and clothed where before they went hungry and naked.'

Only one major hitch hampered the construction of the line. A viaduct had to be built near where the Quagmire bridge crosses the Owenycree River, and a large cutting was undertaken nearby at Bower. These operations delayed the completion of the line by about two months.

The Killarney Junction Railway was unique in several respects. It was one of the cheapest railways in Ireland or Britain in terms of construction cost at around £5,000 per mile. Its annual revenue came to £450 per mile in its first years and from the outset its shareholders received a dividend of five per cent per annum. So economical was the entire venture that the company took the unusual step of reducing its share capital from £375,000 to £225,000 in 1851. It was also one of the earliest lines in Ireland to be completed at the same time as its associated telegraph line - and it was the proprietor of Ireland's first railway-owned hotel.

The GSWR had for some time wanted to develop a 'Grand Hotel' outside of Dublin, and Killarney now appeared to be an attractive location for this enterprise. But they would require 40 acres of land at the rail head and they wanted it free.

Lord Kenmare was not exactly short of land. He owned thousands of acres stretching from the Lakes of Killarney back to Kenmare. But the piece the railway company wanted was special, as it included a magnificent garden which he had lovingly developed over many years. He was most reluctant to part with this land and tried to convince the railway company to site its terminus elsewhere. They were having none of this, however, and a stand-off developed with neither side willing to budge.

Eventually, however, over a late night of cigars and port, I suspect, a compromise was reached. The railway company would get the land it wanted, but the directors agreed that Lord Kenmare and his family could travel free on their railway whenever they liked and that they would delay the departure of the train if any of the Brownes (the Kenmare family) was a little late in arriving at the station. This fine tradition of matching the departure time of the train with the requirements of travellers has been practised ever since with the authority for arranging the synchronisation passing from the Earls of Kenmare to the manager, for the time being, of the Railway (later to become the Great Southern) Hotel. Thc late Jimmy Cullinane, a long serving employee of the Great Southern, recalled that when an Earl of Kenmare arrived late for a train in the 1960s, the Station Manager telephoned Mallow Station and asked that the Cork train be delayed until the Earl could arrive by car. He was duly driven to Mallow by his chauffeur and boarded the train for Dublin.

On that memorable night when the deal was done of course, the objective was to secure the construction of the railway line - but it also paved the way for the birth of a great hotel.

Chapter 3

CHAPTER 3

A Great Hotel is Born

The sun shone brightly on the mountains, lakes and town of Killarney on 16th July 1853.

The townspeople had been anticipating the day for several years, and now it had finally arrived.

Up to a few days previously, teams of workers were putting the finishing touches to the railway station, but now the platform was smooth and clean and built to precisely the correct height, while the 'permanent way' stretched out of the town as far as the eye could see, two parallel iron tracks, that seemed to merge as they reached the horizon.

Very early on that morning a group of distinguished Victorian gentlemen boarded the train at the elegant Kingsbridge Station in Dublin, designed by the great architect John Skelton Mulvany. They included Lord Carlisle, the Lord Lieutenant of Ireland, personal representative of Queen Victoria and effective ruler of the country. He was joined by the Directors of the Great Southern and Western Railway Company, and they were on their way to inaugurate the new railway line to Killarney.

Their journey through Leinster took the party through familiar territory as the puffing steam engine towed its carriages through the stations of Kildare and Portlaoise and on to Thurles and Mallow. From that point however, all was new. Over the previous three years, hundreds or perhaps thousands of men had worked with pick and shovel to clear and level land, cut through hills and build bridges over rivers and streams to create a level platform on which the railway lines could be laid. They were followed by teams who cut railway sleepers

Jarveys await the arrival of the train at Killarney (the Railway Hotel is in the background)
(Lawrence Collection, National Library of Ireland)

The entrance hall to the Railway Hotel

from massive oak trees and laid them in long lines at precise distances, those who erected gates at crossings, who built stations and platforms, signal boxes and water towers, who laid in stocks of coal, who printed tickets and who devised timetables and finally the critical teams who laid the iron rails and bolted them to the sleepers in preparation for this first train.

The journey from Dublin that day took more than nine hours. The train stopped at almost every station, partly so that the Lord Lieutenant could greet waiting crowds but also because the engine needed to take on coal and water.

The passengers may well have been tired and weary as they finally reached their destination, but would have been instantly revived by the scene that greeted them. An estimated 1,500 people had gathered at the railway station which was bedecked with flags, bunting and a large picture of Queen Victoria. A band played as the Lord Lieutenant alighted from the train and was greeted by a Welcoming Committee of local business people.

Almost unnoticed, some fifty other passengers also stepped onto the platform and made their way to the knot of hotel porters who were waiting at the entrance. They were the very first tourists of the steam age to visit Killarney and were quietly conveyed without fuss or favour to one of the six hotels which had focused their attention on providing accommodation for visitors - the Victoria, The Lake Hotel, the Muckross Hotel and O'Sullivan's Hotel, all of which overlooked the lakes, and the Kenmare Arms and Innisfallen hotels which were in the town.

While these were the first passengers to travel from Dublin to Killarney, they were not the first to travel by this means from Dublin to Kerry. A few months earlier, on 16th May 1853, a large party of GS and WR and Killarney Junction Railway officials travelled by train from Dublin to Rathmore. There they had to leave the train, however, as the Bower Cutting was not yet complete, so they proceeded to Killarney by horse-drawn carriage.

In his address at the Railway Station, Lord Carlisle referred in glowing terms to the fine building which was taking shape behind his back. Work was already advanced on the Railway Hotel, Killarney, which would be the flagship of the Railway Company and which would become the first hotel to be owned by a railway company in Britain or Ireland.

The Garden Room at the Railway Hotel showing gaslights

The Billiard Room at the Railway Hotel

As yet, however, it was a building site, so the official party had dinner at the Kenmare Arms Hotel where the manager welcomed them and said that the town was looking forward to an influx of visitors for the Royal Irish Agricultural Show which was to be held in Killarney in the following month. The railway directors responded by offering to carry all Show traffic to Killarney free of charge on both the GS and WR and KJR lines.

Walking stick vendor at the Gap of Dunloe

The idea of providing hotels at major railway stations originated in England where the first great Railway Hotels were built around 1800. The Great Southern and Western Railway Company was anxious to do likewise in Ireland and saw Killarney as its first opportunity to build a hotel. The arrangement with Lord Kenmare provided an ideal site of around 40 acres, adjacent to the railway station, close to the town and within easy reach of the Lakes. The GS and WR saw the Killarney Junction Railway Company, in which it had a sizeable stake, as the ideal vehicle to build the hotel and, with just a little prompting, the Board of KJRC initiated the project almost as soon as they began to construct the railway.

The Killarney Railway Junction Company, whose chairman was James Pennefather, decided at an early stage to hold a limited competition for the design of the hotel. An invitation was extended to some of the leading architects in Britain and Ireland to submit plans and this was met with an excellent response with six designs submitted by the closing date. An expert committee examined the designs and declared William Atkins to be the winner. A well known designer of public buildings, he had previously won a competition to design Cork City Hall, but failed to get the subsequent commission. He was out of luck again in Killarney, however, for the hotel developers failed to commission him to design the Railway Hotel and instead gave the job to Frederick Darley, then aged 55 and at the height of his powers. Born in Dublin in 1798, he is said to have been a pupil of Francis Johnston, the most famous of the early 19th Century Irish architects. He had already designed Merchants Hall in Dublin which was built in 1821, the Kings Inn Library in 1826, a Magnetic Observatory at Trinity College, Dublin and was the official architect to Trinity College since 1834.

Undeterred by the disappointment of winning two architectural competitions and receiving neither commission, William Atkins decided to try again two years later when he again won a competition for a design of Limerick's New Market. Once again, however, the commission went to another architect. Atkins was related through marriage to the Herbert family of Muckross House, but again he was passed over when it came to designing their mansion. This commission went to William Burns, a Scotsman, probably at the prompting of the wife of H.A.Herbert, who was a Scot and who had employed mainly Scottish stewards on her Killarney estate. The luckless Atkins had some consolation, however, in winning a commission to design the entrance gates to Muckross, most of the farm buildings and the church at Muckross Village. He also designed a memorial to Henry Herbert who died in 1886. This took the form of a Celtic High Cross erected in Killeagy cemetery on a site which commanded a view of the entire property.

The reasons why the Killarney Junction Railway Company declined to award the commission for the design of the Railway Hotel to the winner of their own competition, are unclear. A commentary in the British journal *The Builder* in 1853 suggests that Atkins's hotel may have been too elaborate, but politics may also have been involved. *The Builder* merely comments that the commission went to Frederick Darley 'for reasons we do not know'.

Darley's concept of the hotel was on a grand scale and was influenced by some of the great English Victorian hotels in Brighton, Bath and Bournemouth as well as by Martin Burke's Shelbourne Hotel in Dublin which was built in 1825. Unlike the Shelbourne and some of the most famous Dublin hotels, which had been converted from Town Houses, the new Railway Hotel at Killarney was to be purpose-built on a greenfield site and would incorporate the very latest technology.

Darley had been a prominent figure in the 'Tudor Revival' style which was popular in the mid 19th Century. This was typified by square-headed and hooded opes, diamond pattern window panes and tall chimneys. For the Railway Hotel in Killarney, however, he returned to a classical style.

The design combined Victorian elegance and respectability with an array of modern services, comforts and conveniences. It was a solid, stone, square ,squat building, the principal ornamentation of which was a portico fronting the entrance hall.

Jeremy Williams in his book *A Companion Guide to Architecture in Ireland 1837-1921* says that the exterior of the building was 'quiet neo-Georgian with the architectural gestures reserved for the interior where they do not have to contend with Kerry's climate'.

'The progress from the hall, through foyers and reception rooms to the Corinthian-columned grandeur of the dining room focused on a generously curved south-facing bay, is still the most impressive of its kind in Ireland', he writes.

The original design provided for 100 bedrooms which was the largest in any hotel outside the capital. Most of the rooms were small by today's standards, but almost half had interconnecting doors with the adjoining room so that families could book two or more adjacent bedrooms for children and servants. Depending on which contemporary account is believed, the hotel had ten or twelve sitting rooms, all located on the first floor. These could also be hired by guests for their own private use, but in practice most were open to all residents of the hotel. The most innovative feature of the hotel was a very large Coffee Room measuring 70 feet by 24 feet, located along the west side of the building. This was designed as a communal area where residents could meet and chat and it was flanked on either side by two drawing rooms, one for gentlemen and the other for ladies. In practice, however, the ladies were quick to commandeer the coffee room as well, a fact noted by Mrs S. C. Hall in the edition of her *Irish Guide* published in 1856.

Kitchens at the Railway Hotel

Kingsbridge Station Dublin, starting point for the train to Killarney *(Lawrence Collection, National Library of Ireland)*

Other innovations incorporated in the design included an 'airing room' in which guests who had been duly soaked by one of Killarney's 'soft days' could have their clothing dried out, and a large livery stable to the rear which kept 40 horses for hire. The hotel was to be lit by gas and the design included ornate gasoliers for the public rooms as well as provision for small gas works in the grounds. The bedrooms, however, were not gas lit but guests were provided with candles and candlesticks which were lit each evening by members of staff. Most bedrooms also had fire places and again porters were given the responsibility of lighting and maintaining the coal fires which involved filling brass scuttles with coal in a shed to the rear and carrying them several flights of stairs to the bedrooms.

The hotel was also equipped with that most Victorian of luxuries, the Turkish Bath, towards which the GS and WR contributed £1,000.

Before any such service could be rendered however, the hotel had to be built and made ready for its first guests. The building contractor employed more than 300 men at various stages of the construction. These were days when the aftermath of the Famine of 1847-48 remained a grim reality for much of the rural population of Ireland. Entire families had been wiped out and many more had experienced death and emigration. Many of those who survived did so because the menfolk managed to earn some money from the famine works initiated by Lord Kenmare and other local landlords. These were also the days which followed Catholic Emancipation and one of the projects which immediately followed the Famine in Killarney was the resumption of the building of the Catholic Cathedral in the town.

Work on this project was followed almost immediately by the construction of the Railway Hotel which provided further employment opportunities for hundreds of local men. The vast majority of local workers were labourers, although the area boasted some highly skilled stone masons who worked alongside tradesmen from Dublin and England who came to build the new hotel in Killarney.

The Garden Room prepared for dinner *(Lawrence Collection, National Library of Ireland)*

Initially the workforce was mainly local as the task began of excavating the site and laying the foundations. Much to the disappointment of Lord Kenmare the excavation involved the removal of specimen trees and rare tropical plants which he had nurtured, but the architect also managed to preserve part of the garden.

As the work of building the outer shell of the hotel began, specialist tradesmen were hired. They included stone masons who carefully selected each piece of stone and cut it into the desired shape, using only a hammer and chisel. The frontage of the hotel was built of granite quarried in Wicklow, which *The Builder* noted in 1854, 'has been procured at considerable expense.'

As the outer walls rose, scaffolding made from poles lashed together with rope, was erected. Stones were hauled to the scaffolding using block and tackle and fastened into place by the masons. Lentils and sills for the windows were cut and shaped on the site and a small ledge was placed at the divide between the first and upper floors. Eventually the building grew to its full height of three storeys and it was topped off with a balustrade set back from the topmost ledge.

Now it was the turn of the carpenters to cut, shape and place the large roof trusses, nailing each into place, ready for the slaters to cover in the roof with more than 13,000 slates.

During this operation however, part of the new building collapsed. *The Builder* reported on Saturday 29th October 1853 that 'a considerable portion of the Terminus (Railway) Hotel, Killarney, now in the process of erection, has fallen'. The accident happened at night when a part of the building which was being roofed crumbled. Fortunately no workers were present at the time. *The Builder* goes on to report that 'this is the second time a portion of the building has fallen' adding that locals believed the accidents to be caused by the 'insecurity of the foundations'.

Work began immediately on re-building the walls and once the building had been insulated from the elements, the carpenters could return to divide the three storeys with floors and ceilings while the masons built stairways and the plumbers inserted more than a mile of piping through which hot and cold water could be conveyed to bathrooms, kitchens and sculleries. The idea of providing plumbing in bedrooms for toiletry or washing purposes would never have even occurred to Victorians.

The building now approached the stage where it could begin to become a hotel. The large, cavernous kitchen, with its slate floor, could be fitted with coal fired stoves and ovens, large iron baths could be installed in the guest bathrooms on each floor and the decorators could move in to bring Frederick Darley's concept to final fruition.

No public building of the Victorian age would be complete without its ornate ceilings and so a firm of Italian plasterwork artists was commissioned to create floral cornices and centre pieces in the entrance hall, coffee room, drawing rooms and dining room. Carpets were commissioned from Co. Cork and special glass screens were designed for the coffee room so that lady guests could sit behind them in a peaceful draught-proof environment while they chatted or attended to their needle work.

Finally all of the million things which contribute to the fabric of a hotel were put in place. More than 130 beds were ordered from a Dublin manufacturer as well as 150 feather mattresses, 100 commodes and wash stands, 200 water ewers, 110 wardrobes, 130 chests of drawers and 140 rugs, 1,000 linen sheets, bolsters and pillow cases and 200 bedspreads - all for the bedrooms. The Coffee Room alone had 40 tables and 120 chairs while the drawing rooms were furnished with leather and fabric upholstered arm chairs and chaise-longues. The requirements of the dining room included 40 tables, 120 chairs, 300 linen table cloths, 500 napkins, 100 candle sticks, 200 sets of crockery and more than 1,500 pieces of cutlery. All of this was in addition to staff uniforms, kitchen and laundry equipment, hay and straw for the horses and much more. The principal beneficiaries of this spending spree were a Messrs Jones of Dublin who supplied most of the furnishings and Messrs Glenton of London who supplied all of the ironmongery.

As the hotel neared completion, gardeners who had worked for Lord Kenmare were employed to incorporate what remained of the original garden into the grounds of the hotel. They created paths among the ferns and flower beds, built ornamental fountains and grew hedges with recesses to accommodate garden seats.

The original budget for the building was £6,000, but in August 1854 *The Builder* reported that 'we are credibly informed that £18,000 is nearer the sum incurred in its erection'. Some later documents put the final bill, including site costs and furnishings, at around £50,000, but this seems to be an exaggeration. Nevertheless many a modern client could relate to the cost over-run which was involved.

The Coffee Room at the Railway Hotel
(Lawrence Collection, National Library of Ireland)

Early on in the construction the directors of the Killarney Junction Railway Company, which was building the hotel, decided to recruit a manager. After interviewing several experienced hoteliers they awarded the position to Louis Schill, a German who had worked in several leading hotels in Europe and who had owned a hotel in London. He arrived in Killarney late in 1853 and spent the following months working with the architect. They agreed on furnishings, décor and equipment and Louis Schill did much of the ordering, using his knowledge and experience to source high quality fittings and equipment. As the building neared completion he began the process of hiring staff, bringing some experienced Germans to work as waiters and chefs, and supervisors from some Dublin hotels. He also hired more than 150 local people, principally young boys and girls who were trained in a wide variety of jobs including hall, room and kitchen porters, page boys, boot boys, public room, stairs bedroom and scullery maids, pot boys, chefs, butchers, bakers, stokers, launderers, storemen, cellarmen, waiters, waitresses, farriers and gas makers. All were given uniforms and placed under the watchful eye of strict supervisors who inspected each employee every day for cleanliness and who instructed them in obedience, etiquette, good manners and a deferential attitude to guests. In return staff were provided with meals, some were accommodated in the hotel and all received pay which was just a little better than that given to domestic servants.

With the final gilt mirror in place, the last brass rail polished, the staff drilled and inspected and the larder brimming over with Kerry mutton and Killarney salmon, Louis Schill was ready to receive his first guests.

The long life of the Railway Hotel had begun.

Corner of the coffee lounge at the Railway Hotel

Chapter 4

CHAPTER 4

Victoria Rules the Lakes

The Railway Hotel, Killarney, opened in 1854 without any of the pomp and circumstance which had surrounded the opening of the railway a year earlier.

The Directors, headed by James Pennefather, chairman of the Killarney Junction Railway Company, contented themselves with a dinner at which they entertained a few, well chosen, friends including the High Sheriff of County Cork, M. McCarthy O'Leary, 'three or four gentlemen connected with the Press', William Chayter, the company secretary and Board Members M.J. O'Connell, T. Gallwey, E. Cane, P.R.Guinness, T. Darley, S. Hardy, W.M. Barrington, W. Haughton, E.E. Illbury, V. O'Connor and a 'Mr Jones'.

We have to thank one of the 'three or four gentlemen connected with the press' for details of what was described as ' a social and pleasant evening'. 'We sat down to an entertainment so well cooked and served as to augur most favourably the future success of the establishment in the culinary department', wrote the editor of one Killarney newspaper, and then in the best traditions of his profession, he neglects to record anything about the food served, but recalls that 'the wines, champagne, burgundy, claret, port and sherry were of the best vintages.'

'There was no regular drinking of toasts', he reports in a style not a million miles from that of *Hello!*, 'but in the course of the night, Mr Gallwey proposed, in a short and humorous speech, the health of Mr Pennefather and the Directors, which was responded to in the same strain by that gentleman, who concluded by proposing the healths of Mr. McCarthy O'Leary and the other guests, to which Mr McCarthy O'Leary responded. Subsequently Mr Haughton, one of the Directors, in very complementary terms, gave the health of Mr Chayter, the secretary, to which that gentleman fitly (sic) responded. The Chairman also proposed the Press, for which Mr Raymond of the *Kerry Evening Post* very briefly returned thanks.'

Little wonder that all this toasting with burgundy, clarets and ports might dim the recollection of the assembled hacks. But 'Mr Raymond' of the *Kerry Evening Post* had taken his notes and adds at the conclusion of his report:

'We had almost forgotten that the Railway Directors have erected, for the use of their own premises, hotel and terminus, a Gasometer in which gas was generated on Monday last, for the first time, and with which the hotel was most efficiently lighted during the night. The Gasoliers in the coffee room, when lighted, presented a most brilliant effect.'

It did not take long for the local gentry and business community to flock to the Railway Hotel for balls and dinners. They were a colourful lot, rich and idle and they chose the hotel as an alternative to the endless round of house parties in their mansions.

Maurice O'Leary, writing in *The Kerryman* in 1953 conjured up the scene.

'For a vignette of the opening of the hotel, one must try to imagine the Victorian scene. The arrival of the carriages brought the ladies in their voluminous finery and the gentlemen in their long dress coats, stiff white

Queen Victoria at Ross Castle *(Illustrated London News)*

fronts and collars and long, narrow-fitting trousers. The reception, with its rigid formality and absolute deference to polite procedure, the toasts, with that of "The Queen" in pride of place, and the rhetoric of the speeches, were all part of the occasion. Beneath the gas light and the sparkling chandeliers moved sedate figures, the ladies perhaps, finding the sanctuary of the drawing room and their menfolk seeking the refuge of the smoking room or the billiard room, to relax and smoke and talk as men will, when ladies are not present. The golden sovereign held sway and of the might of the almighty dollar, little had yet been heard. England had become a great industrial power, enormously wealthy and the English aristocrat and captain of industry was the chief tourist in Killarney.'

Glittering occasions there were and English industrialists also, but not enough of them favoured the Railway Hotel with their business for the company to make ends meet.

Louis Schill was accustomed to running what would now be called 'luxury hotels' and set high standards which in turn created high overheads. Within only a few months of the Railway Hotel opening, it became obvious to the directors that it was going to incur heavy losses which would have to be supported by additional investment. And that is what the Killarney Junction Railway Company was not prepared to do.

Henry Arthur Herbert (1815-1866) of Muckross House and his wife Mary Herbert

Within six years of the hotel opening the Directors decided to call it a day and quietly sold the Railway Hotel to the Great Southern and Western Railway Company around 1859. Louis Schill, who had commented that he had been surprised 'at the high cost of running the house', packed his bags, boarded the train which had delivered his first guests, and returned to London where he continued to work as a highly respected hotel manager.

The Directors of the Great Southern and Western Railway Company were not at all pleased to be landed again with the hotel they had tried to run by proxy. Their business was steam engines and iron rails and robust mechanics and they rightly decided that they did not want to get involved with anything as foppish as the day to day operation of a hotel. They looked around for a solution and found it in the person of John Dunn, who for many years had been House Steward to the Earl of Kenmare. Prudent, efficient, well known and respected by the local gentry, Mr Dunn was proposed by the son of his erstwhile employer as a possible tenant of the Railway Hotel. The Directors heaved a communal sigh of relief after they had negotiated a deal under which John Dunn would pay them a rent of £900 per annum, a sum which might be commanded by a large commercial building in Dublin, but which was regarded as exceptionally high for a 'seasonal' hotel in the wilds of Kerry.

Yet the formidable Mr Dunn seems not only to have made ends meet but became quite a wealthy man in the process. He reduced costs, employed fewer staff and closed the hotel from September to May, apart from special occasions when it was opened for banquets.

But fate was to smile on the House Steward of Lord Kenmare, on the Railway Hotel and on the entire Killarney area, in the unlikely form of Royalty.

Victoria was the last great Queen of England. She ruled over an Empire which included Ireland, and she was genuinely admired and even loved by a large number of her subjects. Although she owed her crown indirectly to the refusal of an English nobleman to marry the Kerry woman that he loved (see *Parknasilla - The Centenary Book*), she was also very popular in Ireland and indeed in the 'Kingdom' of Kerry. Victoria was quiet, conservative and grumpy by nature, and not easily amused. Her travels therefore were limited and for most of her reign she had never been to Ireland. Much lobbying was undertaken at the Court of St James to persuade Her Majesty to visit the Emerald Isle. This was done for both political and economic reasons. A Royal Visit would strengthen loyalty to The Crown and would create interest in Ireland among City of London investors and perhaps even the growing numbers of Britons who were now travelling beyond their shores by steamer, principally to France.

Queen Victoria meets members of the Herbert family. *(Illustrated London News).*

Among the most active lobbyists was Lord Kenmare who believed that a Royal Visit to his scenic estate around the Lakes of Killarney would be a powerful means of attracting visitors. Victoria, however, remained unamused and it was a good five years before the Irish lobby had any success. This came in the form of a visit to Ireland by Edward, Prince of Wales in 1858. He arrived in Dublin where he was well received and made his way by train to Killarney where he spent all of eight days touring the countryside and lodging at both the Victoria Hotel and Muckross House. In his book *Echo After Echo* Donal Horgan writes that 'the Prince seems to have enthusiastically entered into the spirit of the occasion by bounding up CorranTuathaill and Mangerton, closely followed, it should be said, by an army of reporters who diligently recorded his every movement and utterance.'

As a royal and media event however, the visit of Prince Edward was little more than a curtain raiser for the biggest Royal Spectacular to be held in Ireland since the Battle of the Boyne. Almost six years after the idea was first mooted Victoria was persuaded to visit that part of her Kingdom that lay beyond the Irish Sea. Elaborate preparations were made for the visit and for the best part of a year leading up to the scheduled date, Dublin Castle was in a state of jitters. The Lord Lieutenant and his advisers knew quite well the state of incipient rebellion which always existed in the country and they used every informer and spy on their books to seek out plots of disruption or even assassination. They need not have worried, for even though she was the English Monarch, Victoria was popular throughout the country and the economy which she led had brought a level of prosperity to the plain people of Ireland which they had not enjoyed for more than a century. Any violent demonstrations therefore would not command popular support and those who would lead such actions decided to keep their powder dry.

Victoria with her husband Prince Albert, their children and a large entourage arrived in Kingstown on a warm August day to be greeted by a crowd estimated to be around 200,000. The harbour town was festooned with bunting, with many of Dublin's wealthiest families watching her arrival from the balconies and lawns of their terraced houses facing the sea.

On Tuesday 27th August 1861 the Royal party boarded a train at Kingsbridge at 12.55pm and, according to contemporary accounts, arrived in Killarney at 6.30pm. If these reports are true the Great Southern and Western Railway company must have pulled out all the stops, for only a year earlier it was proudly announcing an express train journey of 'only eight hours' between Dublin and Killarney. Cutting the time to only five and a half hours in a single year seems to have been a remarkable achievement.

The railway station at Killarney was once again 'en fete' and this time the decorations extended to the Railway Hotel. The welcoming party was headed by Victoria's two principal hosts, the Earl of Castlerosse (Lord

'Three Cheers for Her Majesty', Victoria visits the Lakes of Killarney *(Illustrated London News)*

Ella's reference to the stag hunt does not, however, tell the full story. Local folklore has it that the stag, which had been captured days earlier, so that it could be released, chased and killed, made good its escape a few hours before the Queen arrived and that the whole event had to be faked, with lots of shouting, horn blowing and galloping about after an imaginary animal.

Whatever the real story of Victoria's visit to Killarney, it turned out to be a magnificent publicity coup for the town. The press pack, having no real story to write, let their imaginations run riot in their descriptions of the magnificence of Killarney and its environs. They coined the phrase 'Ladies View' for a spot on the road to Moll's Gap where ladies of the Royal Party stopped to take in the view and they waxed eloquently about how enraptured Victoria and her family had been, how welcoming were the people of Kerry and what splendid hotels could be found in the town. Singled out for special mention were the Victoria and Railway hotels, where no doubt, the management had looked after the scribblers very well indeed.

Victoria not only put Killarney on the map as a 'must see' destination for her self-respecting subjects, but she also did a very good selling job for Ireland. 'If Her Majesty could travel on the new steamships and new trains to visit a remote corner of the Emerald Isle, why could we not also do so?' was a proposition put by many a Victorian wife to her well-to-do husband. And as the only possible answer was 'Why not ?', the first real tourism market was opened for Ireland - one which remains our largest market to-day.

Chapter 5

CHAPTER 5

Nobility, Tourists and Refugees

The publicity generated by the visit of Queen Victoria paid off. Suddenly Ireland became fashionable among the British Victorians who, being highly fashion-conscious, began to cross the Irish Sea in growing numbers to sample the social life of Dublin, the genteel elegance of Kingstown and the wilderness of Killarney.

The train journey from Dublin to Killarney had been cut to less than seven hours and it was now also possible to visit the town from Tralee, thanks to the Tralee and Killarney Railway which was sanctioned in 1853 and opened on 18th July 1859. This additional spur was built by a separate company whose capital was subscribed by the Killarney Junction Railway Company. Once again the contract for building this line was awarded to William Dargan, but the construction was delayed when workers objected to their wages of seven and a half pence (less than 3c) per day and staged a strike. They soon returned to work without an increase and work resumed, only to be delayed again when the railway company ran out of money. The project was further beset by ill fortune when a deep cutting at Coolcorcoran near Killarney caved in on 29th August 1857, resulting in the death of three workmen and injuries to several others. Eventually the line was completed and opened on Saturday 16th July 1859, when the GS and WR Directors once again travelled down from Dublin. This time they stayed in the Railway Hotel and relaxed in the Turkish Bath towards which they had contributed £1,000.

Because of engineering considerations, the line from Tralee does not actually pass through Killarney station, which is located at the end of a 300 yard stub where the line terminates. As a result trains arriving from Mallow must back out before continuing their journey to Tralee while Mallow-bound trains must back into the station.

In 1860, the year before Victoria's visit, the Great Southern and Western Railway took over both the Killarney and Tralee Junction Railway Companies, including the Killarney Railway Hotel. The GS and WR had invested large sums in both companies and was a major shareholder. Nevertheless the local investors, including a number of Killarney land owners and merchants, were well rewarded for their enterprise and showed a handsome profit on their investment.

Employees of the GS and WR seem to have been well rewarded too.
In his book *One Hundred and Fifty Years of Irish Railways*, Fergus Mulligan describes the state of the GS and WR in 1860.

'It had built 350 track miles and was well on the way to establishing itself as one of the best run railways in the country. Morale among staff was high, for employment prospects on the railway were good and the men took pride in their work. Wages were above average and even then clerical staff worked only an eight hour day. For unskilled workers there was a thirteen hour day. Even so, with an average of ten trains a day passing through, life in a country station should not be compared with a cotton mill or a steel works. There was plenty

Street scene , Killarney *(Lawrence Collection, National Library of Ireland)*

of opportunity for extra-curricular activities., some of which landed the participants in trouble. For example, the station masters at Thurles and Templemore were severely reprimanded for slipping off to Cashel together for a flutter on the races during slack periods. Worse, they had travelled by train without paying their fare! Other distractions were dogs, cards, gaming and of course the demon drink. The company issued repeated notices and threats of fines, suspension or dismissal for anyone found under the influence. While specifically forbidding staff to keep pigs or goats in their cottages, it was generous in response to dedicated service and in welfare schemes was well ahead of its time.'

Fergus Mulligan goes on to describe some of the delights experienced by train travellers en route to the Killarney Railway Hotel:

'The route is through wild and beautiful country, with gorse bushes brushing against the carriage window as the train hurtles through jagged limestone cuttings, with the Kerry mountains as a backdrop. There is a number of stops on the way at beautifully-kept little stations in the middle of nowhere where a few people get on and get off. It is a constant amazement to find the brassy commercialism of Killarney in the middle of this wild and lonesome beauty.'

The Railway Hotel was immediately visible to passengers arriving in this town of 'brassy commercialism'. Porters from the hotel awaited the arrival of guests on the platform, and 'front of house' staff, in their bright red and gold uniforms could be seen, standing at the hotel's entrance. Porters from other Killarney hotels were obliged to keep their distance outside the railway station and were not allowed enter the platform which was the private property of the railway company. What Maurice O'Leary of *The Kerryman* described in a 1953 article as 'a minor war' broke out between the Railway Hotel and its principal competitors. John O'Leary, proprietor of the Royal Victoria Hotel, placed an advertisement in local and national newspapers declaring:

'It is necessary to inform tourists that the Railway Company, proprietors of the Terminus Hotel in the town, send upon the platform as TOUTERS for their hotel, the porters, boatmen, car drivers and guides in their employment, and exclude the servants of the hotels on the lake. They will however be found in waiting at the Station door.'

The fact that John O'Leary referred to the Railway Hotel as the 'Terminus Hotel' gives some indication of the depth of feeling behind the advertisement. There was a strong suggestion in the word that the hotel was far removed from the scenic attractions of the Lakes.

It is not clear if the Railway Hotel management was in fact touting for business among arriving passengers, but if such was the case, it was certainly not unusual in the late 19th century when the practice of booking accommodation in advance was not very common. As a result, porters and other staff from competing hotels would congregate at railway stations all over the country seeking to win business from arriving passengers. The station master at Broadstone in Dublin received regular complaints from arriving passengers who were harried by porters representing the 22 hotels in the vicinity. Competition at Killarney may not have been as intense but there were reports of hotel representatives boarding the train at Mallow and approaching passengers in the carriages during the final stages of their journey.

The 'hotel war' seems to have eased by 1865, however. The ubiquitous Mr and Mrs S. C. Hall in their guide published that year report that 'The Railway Company have made a very judicious arrangement, by which only one attendant from each of the hotels is permitted to enter the Station on the arrival of the train.'

But the GS and WR went on to incur the further wrath of Killarney hoteliers by devising a schedule which brought the last train of the day to Killarney at 9.30pm. By this time, the hoteliers claimed, passengers were too tired to travel on to the hotels around the lake and instead opted for the convenient comforts of the Railway Hotel, adjacent to the station.

By this time John Dunn appears to have given up his lease on the hotel, for the manager who greeted the Halls in 1865 was a 'Mr C. Goodman'. This worthy gentleman was manager of the Sackville Street Club in Dublin and is mentioned as such in an advertisement for the hotel which appeared in the Hall's guide called *A Week in Killarney*. The advertisement, which provides an interesting insight into the operation of the business at that time, begins with a dubious address for the hotel as 'Lakes of Killarney' and goes on to describe the premises as: 'This magnificent Establishment, admitted to be one of the finest in Europe, possesses everything requisite to promote the comfort and convenience of the Nobility and Tourists'.

The hotel, says the advertisement, contains

'One Hundred Bedrooms, a Noble Coffee Room, a Drawing Room for Ladies and Families, Several Elegant and handsomely furnished Sitting Rooms, Billiard and Smoking Room, Baths etc. etc.'

Readers were advised (in very small print) that 'the charges will be found moderate'.

Mr Goodman also took care to emphasise the unique selling points of the hotel.

'The Porters of the Hotel await the arrival of each train, for the removal of luggage etc.'
Nor was the cuisine forgotten.

'Table d'Hote at Half Past Six O'Clock' appeared in strong bold type, and underneath, in much smaller type the

Farm scene near Killarney in the 1880s (Lawrence Collection, National Library of Ireland)

hotel explained that 'for the convenience of commercial gentlemen, a room has been established for their accommodation'.

Rival hotelier John O'Leary's advertisement complaining about the porter situation, also referred to 'boatmen, car drivers and guides employed by the (Terminus) hotel', and Mr Goodman's advertisement confirms all of this. 'Posting- Boats, cars, carriages and Ponies at fixed moderate rates', it says, adding that 'Boatmen and Drivers are paid ample wages with the express understanding that they are not to annoy Visitors by soliciting for money.'

Today's Killarney hoteliers will empathise with the problems encountered by Mr Goodman in filling his hotel in the off season. He hints at these in his advertisement with the line: 'Parties taken as boarders at a moderate charge from 1st November to June.'

He rounds it all off with a little piece of self-promotion, declaring in large bold capital letters: 'CONTINENTAL LANGUAGES SPOKEN BY THE MANAGER'.

Mr Goodman may have needed the further qualification of diplomacy two years later when his hotel was invaded by a large group of highly stressed landed gentry. In the previous months the Fenian Movement had gained momentum in Kerry with leaders calling for a new rebellion against English Rule and groups of men training and drilling in the valleys and glens around Killarney, barely out of sight of roaming Victorian tourists.

In February 1867 the Fenians of Cahirciveen were reported to be on the march towards Killarney. The rumour mill was cranked up to fever pitch and with every day the reported numbers of the march grew, from an initial handful to 'an army of thousands'. Reports of burning and pillage reached the houses of the gentry along the route and large numbers decided that discretion was the better part of valour and 'fled for their lives', taking with them their families, jewellery and, as a contemporary report put it, 'their plate'.

This terrified band of wealthy refugees made Killarney their rendezvous and 'swarmed into the Railway Hotel, where chaos prevailed'. From the sanctuary of the Coffee Room they sent messages to the military seeking help and in due course a large force of Redcoats also took up residence in the hotel, posted sentries around the perimeter and prepared the building to withstand a siege.

They need not have worried themselves because the great Fenian march never came to much. At best it swelled to a hundred incipient rebels, but most abandoned the enterprise in the face of the threat of attack by the military and the whole thing petered out.

Nevertheless, the Cahirciveen Fenians did achieve something by scaring some of the most powerful families in Kerry to fly to Killarney for protection. The episode resulted in the families being held up to ridicule in several ballads, including 'The Killarney Scare' by T.D. O'Sullivan which describes a terrified horseman flogging his animal at break-neck speed through the streets of Killarney as if thousands of blood-thirsty Fenians were hard on his heels.

Still onward he urges his foam-spattered steed
O'er the roads, through the street without slackening high speed.
Until rider and horse, driving onward pell-mell
Rush into the porch of the Railway Hotel.

The ballad goes on to describe the scenes inside the hotel:

And then to hear each pale Shoneen, while shaking quick with palpitation
Describe the terrors of the scene that caused his class such consternation
And Oh, to hear the poor poltroons, who long had passed as men of mettle
Each clamouring for his silver spoons and searching for his plated kettle.

All ended well of course and O'Sullivan found a silver lining in the episode for the sheltered young ladies of the Big Houses who were given this unexpected 'short break' in the Railway Hotel with the added bonus of meeting some handsome Redcoats.

What delight for the bright-eyed and timid young belles
Who thought, as they gazed on the red-coated swells
That an annual panic would scarce be amiss
If each would provide them a chance such as this.

After this comic-opera scene the Railway Hotel returned to the more mundane business of catering for the 'Nobility' and 'Tourists', the bulk of its business being from among the latter. It also battled away for market share with the ten other hotels which were then in the town or scattered around the shores of the lakes. By far its most serious competitor was the Victoria Hotel, which preceded the arrival of the railway. The Prince of Wales stayed there and the hotel reminded potential customers of this in its advertisements which invariably stated that it 'Enjoyed the Royal Patronage of the Prince of Wales'. The Railway Hotel could not compete in the

Killarney traffic in 1890 (Lawrence Collection, National Library of Ireland)

royalty stakes. Indeed it was 1899 before it welcomed its first potentate, His Highness the Thakore and Maharani of Goudal.

In his advertisement of 1865, John O'Leary referred to the porters, boatmen, car drivers and guides who touted for business on behalf of the Railway Hotel. These employees were additional to the regular hotel complement of chefs, waiters, chambermaids and others who tendered to the every whim of guests inside the hotel. Both the Railway and Victoria hotels employed a large retinue of staff who provided 'tourist services'. Highest in the pecking order of these were the 'Commodores' of the hotel 'Navies', or boat crews. Jeremiah Clifford was the commodore of the 'Railway Hotel Navy', a crew of 24, described by Mrs Hall as 'all smart and intelligent young men, dressed alike in blue and white'. They manned the hotel boats which took visitors on cruises around the Lakes. Mrs Hall had words of high praise for the Railway Hotel navy and in particular for Jeremiah Clifford whom she described as 'a most pleasant companion, full of knowledge, who can tell a legend with admirable effect and dance an Irish jig as vigorously as the best youth in Kerry'.

Official hotel guides were also well regarded and well paid. Among them were the Spillane Brothers, Tom and Stephen who were attached to the Railway Hotel. In fact it was Stephen who acted as personal guide to the Prince of Wales during his 1858 visit. He may well have worked for the Victoria Hotel at that time as it was there that the Prince stayed.

Tourist services were not confined to the employees of the larger hotels, however. The visitor boom generated a dynamic local industry involving hundreds of people who found hundreds of means of separating the visitors from their pounds, shillings and pence. Up to ten workshops were established in and around Killarney manufacturing gift items and souvenirs from local arbutus wood and bog oak. Dolls and figurines were also produced as well as polished walking sticks made from blackthorn branches. The souvenir shop had not yet arrived, so this merchandise was sold very successfully by young barefoot girls, dressed in colourful dresses and shawls who paraded around the streets of the town and could be found as far afield as the Torc Waterfall and the Gap of Dunloe.

'Mountain Dew Girls' could also be found at these spots selling a concoction of poitin and goats's milk. Add in touters, more than 100 jarveys, freelance guides and an assortment of amateur and professional beggars to get a picture of the bustling tourist town that was Killarney in the last two decades of the 19th century.

Further royalty were to arrive in Killarney before the century ended. The Duke and Duchess of York visited the Earl and Countess of Kenmare and during their visit a proposal was made that the Crown should purchase Muckross House as a Royal Residence but the idea came to nothing.

The idea of building on the success of the Railway Hotel in Killarney did however mature and blossom. In 1894 Great Southern and Western Railway invested in yet another associate company, Southern Hotels, to extend its hotel interests in Kerry. This company, in which once again the local gentry and landowners had shares, was established in 1892. It purchased The Bishop's House at Parknasilla, near Sneem with 114 acres of land from the Bishop of Limerick, Rev. Charles Graves, and opened it as a hotel in 1895. Despite its remote location the Bishop's House did excellent business in its first year, by which time the Southern Hotel Company had embarked on a second venture - a new hotel in Kenmare. James Franklin Fuller, who had designed Ashford Castle in Cong and Tinakilly House in Rathnew was commissioned to design the Kenmare hotel which was completed in 1896. He produced a design which was very modern for its time and even equipped the new hotel with electricity - a remarkable innovation for the 1890s when one realises that many families in the area did not get electricity into their homes until the 1960s. Fuller was also commissioned to replace the Bishop's House at Parknasilla with a brand new hotel. The third hotel in the Southern chain was at Caragh Lake. It was built in 1893 and an advertisement in 1896 claims that 'the hotel has been enlarged and now includes a new coffee room, a smoking room, various sitting rooms and large and lofty bedrooms.' The hotel maintained its own salmon and trout hatchery and offered guests access to 25,000 acres of 'the best shooting'.

As with the Killarney Railway Junction Company, the shareholders in the Southern Hotel Company discovered early on that making profit from seasonal hotels in remote areas of Ireland was a very difficult proposition. The company does not appear to have run up large losses, nor was it threatened with liquidation, but in 1896, the Southern Hotel Company was acquired by the Great Southern and Western Railway Company, and Great Southern Hotels was born. In the following year the hotels at Killarney, Parknasilla, Kenmare and Caragh Lake were branded as 'Great Southern' and the 'Railway Hotel' title faded into history.

As the Gay Nineties ended Killarney was on the crest of a wave, having become one of the most fashionable of Victorian resorts and a bustling prosperous town with a dozen busy hostelries of which the Great Southern Hotel remained the biggest, most modern and best.

Little did anyone think what the new century would bring.

Chapter 6

CHAPTER 6

Victorians - the Smug Posers

So who were these Victorians who were the lifeblood of early tourism in Killarney, in Ireland and in much of Europe?

They did not exist before Victoria ascended the throne in 1837, but they outlived her death in 1901, hanging on until their children sent their grandsons to the trenches in 1914.

They were English mainly, and well-to-do. The population of Great Britain comprised millions of men, women and children, but only a small elite can be classed as Victorians - the ascendancy, of course, and rich merchants, bankers, professionals and industrialists. It was on them and their American cousins, that the Industrial Revolution poured its munificence. For the rest of the population, being a Victorian meant subservience, long working hours and earnings which supported only a very basic lifestyle.

Souvenir sellers at Killarney

An early Irish postcard

A graceious and warm welcome (Don Mac Monagle)

Polite conversation in the lounge (Don Mac Monagle)

Victorians in Britain and in America were mainly 'noveau riche', who had grown wealthy very rapidly on the back of of booming economies fired by new industries, railroads and land speculation. They were smug, moral posers who conveyed their self righteousness and superiority through the formal beards and top hats of their men and the long involuted dresses of the women.

As Robert M. Pirsig remarked in his book 'Lila':

'Smug posing was the essence of their style. That's what the mansions were, poses, turrets and gingerbread and ornamental cast iron. The did it to their bodies with bustles and corsets. They did it to their whole social and psychic lives with impossible proprieties of table manners and speech and posture and sexual repression. Their paintings captured it perfectly, expressionless, mindless, cream-skinned ladies sitting around Greek columns, draped in ancient Greek robes, in perfect form and posture, except for one breast hanging out, which no one noticed, presumably because they were so elevated and so pure.'

These then were the tourists who flocked to Killarney and other parts of Ireland during the mid-19th century and it would be another half century before their employees won the right to paid holidays and could join the elite in Killarney.

Ireland presented a novelty and a challenge to the Victorians - a backward agricultural country with poor roads and a very basic infrastructure outside of the capital city of Dublin. It even had a different system of time, called 'Irish Time' which could be one or two hours ahead or behind the time by which Her Majesty's Clocks were set. This both intrigued and annoyed the Victorians who had developed a phobia for time-keeping and who studied Railway Timetables as if they were the latest work from Charles Dickens. It was not until 1884 that Greenwich Mean Time spread to Ireland and a chronometer, set according to the official time in London,

Queen Victoria, a popular Monarch *(Lawrence Collection, National Library of Ireland)*

Excursion party travelling to the Lakes from the Railway Hotel *(Lawrence Collection, National Library of Ireland)*

was carried by steamer each evening across the Irish Sea to ensure that John Bull's Other Island stepped in time with the rest of the Kingdom.

Irish distances too, perturbed the visitor in Victorian times (and they still do). A mile in Ireland was different to a mile in England with eleven 'Irish miles' being the equal of about fourteen 'English miles'. Bianconi cars and the first railways measured distances according to 'Irish miles', creating considerable confusion among passengers who idled away their travelling hours by calculating times and distances between towns and stations.

Victorians were extremely class conscious, regarding servants and tradesmen as belonging to lower classes. The first Irish railways fed into the attitudes of their customers by creating distinct classes, First, Second and Third, on their trains. Passengers in all three classes arrived at their destination simultaneously, but those in higher classes enjoyed a measure of additional comfort such as cushioned seats and, occasionally, picnic baskets of food.

Even the postal service recognised Victorian class-consciousness with First and Second Class post on offer during the 1880s. Victorians liked to write letters and notes to each other, frequently communicating from their homes in London and other cities by sending servants to and fro between houses carrying notes which were often extremely trivial in nature. The Postcard, when it came into vogue at the turn of the century created a new opportunity for the dissemination of trivialities. At first Her Majesty's Post Office refused to handle postcards which were not enclosed in envelopes on the grounds that their content may be private or personal and open to prying eyes. It relented however in 1902, opening the door for Victorians to deluge each other with cryptic messages along the lines of 'Wish You Were Here'. Everyone was happy - the Victorians who travelled and wanted to boast about it, the Victorians at home who were planning their next journey, the photographers, like Louis Anthony of Killarney who captured images for the postcards, printers like Daniel Mac Monagle and, not least, Her Majesty's Post Office which was handling 60 million postcards as early as 1903.

The Victorians also liked to write in their diaries and the era has left a legacy of personal diaries crammed with trivia. Public diarists emerged also, many of whom wrote down their impressions of travelling in Ireland and had them published. The most popular practitioners were Anna Maria and Samuel Carter Hall who published several editions of their *Irish Guide* and commented regularly and with commendable objectivity on their frequent visits to Killarney. Anna Maria was born in Dublin in 1800, but the family moved soon afterwards to Wexford where she spent her childhood. She married Samuel Hall with whom she wrote several books and guides and the couple also campaigned over many years to alleviate the lot of the poor in Victorian Britain.

The Victorians who visited Ireland saw much poverty and deprivation in the years after the Famine, but appear to have ignored it, just as tourists do in Third World destinations today. Indeed they were usually so busy that they hardly noticed the poor living conditions of the local population. Ever the Busy Bees, Victorians liked to fill their days with activities which would enrich their minds or provide exercise. They had a pre-occupation with health and flocked to spas in Britain and Europe. They visited museums, art galleries and zoos, attended concerts and recitals.

While these enlightening attractions were absent in Killarney, the Victorians made the most of what was on offer. They took photographs with their plate cameras and even developed the films themselves. The Great Southern Hotel in Killarney was one of several hotels equipped with a Dark Room. They trekked over the Gap of Dunloe, went boating on the lakes, took their sketch pads to scenic areas and occasionally participated in fishing, game shooting, horse riding and the stag hunt. From 1900 onwards they began to play golf.

***Victorian elegance** (Don Mac Monagle)*

When they dined in the evening, the Victorians displayed their pre-occupation with table manners. Ladies were escorted into dinner by male companions, served first at table and were expected to eat delicately. Before the port and cigars were served they adjourned to a Drawing Room where they engaged in embroidery and polite conversation. Menfolk were also expected to observe strict etiquette, but could be less inhibited at table when it came to eating heartily. After the meal they drank, smoked and talked before rejoining the ladies.

The food they consumed was simple by today's standards but would alarm any cardiac surgeon. Dinner began with oysters or shell fish, followed by rich, thick soups, another fish course and then large joints of meat which were generally carved at the table, vegetables, potatoes, cheese and several desserts. This evening feast was on top of a similar but less formal lunch, a buffet breakfast comprising cooked and cold meats and fish, breads and beverages, morning coffee and afternoon tea. Lunch and dinner was accompanied by unlimited quantities of wine, principally Claret and Hock.

As visitors, Victorians were fussy and demanding of hotel staff and early providers of tourism services. They tended to watch their pennies and would haggle over the price of refreshments and souvenirs whether these be the magnificent inlaid tables, trays and chairs made by skilled Killarney craftsmen or the milk and poitin sold on the Gap of Dunloe by the 'Mountain Dew Girls'.

Pompous, moralistic and tight-fisted as they were, however, the Victorians were Ireland's first real tourists who made a valuable contribution to a weak post-Famine economy and who initiated a tradition for visiting Killarney which flourishes to-day.

Victorian postcard

Picnic at the Lakes around 1900

Chapter 7

CHAPTER 7

Cameras, Cars and a Handsome Spy

From 1895, Thomas Cook, the British travel agent had included Killarney in its package tour programme and in the following year the first American visitors to travel on an organised tour arrived at the Railway and Royal Victoria hotels.

By 1899 Killarney was basking in a tourism boom with more than 100 jarveys to be seen lined up outside the railway station, more than a dozen hotels and some twenty inns constantly filled with visitors and associated businesses doing a roaring trade.

The Directors of Great Southern Hotels, which in 1899 began to operate as an independent business within the railway company, embarked on a programme of investment which included the renovation of the lounge of the Killarney hotel, completed in 1900 at a cost of £6,000. The opening of this new facility was somewhat marred by a strike of nine waiters, all German, who untied their aprons after a dispute over wages, boarded the train to Dublin and were never seen again in Killarney. The hotel manager reacted by immediately hiring nine local young men who were operating as waiters the following day.

Nor did the refurbishment meet with universal approval. In his book *A Companion Guide to Architecture in Ireland 1837-1921*, Jeremy Williams writes:

'Desperate attempts by earlier managements to speed up its (Great Southern Hotel) tempo have been singularly unsuccessful and indeed there are signs today of a desire to recreate its leisurely reassurance as an interlude between the long train journey across Ireland and the vertiginous jaunts of the jarvey car.'

The refurbishment decision may have been prompted by a worrying downward trend in business. The Great Southern Hotel achieved a turnover of £12,000 in 1900. This fell slightly to £11,876 in 1901, but it was again substantially down to £10, 825 in 1902 and remained under the £11,000 mark up to 1904 when the hotel celebrated its 50th anniversary.

By 1901 the linguistically talented Mr Goodman had moved to pastures new and the Directors once again reverted to the strategy of leasing out the hotels. The franchise was, on this occasion, given to a German hotelier, Franz Koenig, who paid an annual fee for the right to operate the Killarney hotel, an arrangement which in subsequent years was extended to the hotels in Parknasilla, Caragh Lake and Kenmare. He invested in additional furnishings and some of the silverware that he bought is today displayed in the Great Southern Hotel Killarney, bearing his distinctive 'K' crest.

Mr Koenig was a shrewd and entrepreneurial businessman who quickly saw that while the Killarney Great Southern was doing well and attracting wealthy guests, many more passengers arriving on the trains sought more modest accommodation in and around the town.

At his prompting, Great Southern Hotels decided to build a second hotel on its Killarney site. It would offer more basic accommodation than the Great Southern and would not have the same level of facilities. Construction began in 1906 and the hotel, with 100 beds, was opened in the following year, without much ceremony. 'The New Hotel', as it was called, aimed to attract the growing numbers of English working class visitors who could now afford to visit Killarney. Coming on organised tours which were known locally as 'Lancashire Wakes', these good folk could not afford to stay in luxury hotels, but could now stay at 'The New Hotel' just beside the station where they could rub shoulders with the more up-market clientele of the Great Southern. The idea worked well at the beginning with 'The New Hotel' grossing £3,069 in its first year while the 'Great Southern' had a turnover of £11,710. Mr Koenig, in a memo to the directors, noted that Thomas Cook and the London Polytechnic guaranteed the hotel 50 clients per night. He also reported that the Great Southern, which then could sleep about 120 guests per night was frequently overbooked with up to 150 American visitors arriving on some evenings, particularly in the period between July and September. 'We are obliged to sleep out some guests', Mr Koenig reported.

The boom however, did not last. Its first year of 1907 was the best that 'The New Hotel' would enjoy. Turnover in the following year fell from £3,069 to £2,384 and it was 1913 before they again broke the £3,000 mark. To compound the situation turnover at the Great Southern also declined from £11,710 in 1907 to £9,531 in 1908 and as low as £8,216 in 1912. Mr Koenig observed that the emerging pattern was that 'The New Hotel' was merely taking business away from the Great Southern. A significant number of 'tourists' and perhaps even a few 'nobility' recognised the good value offered by 'The New Hotel' and transferred their business while the working class visitors seemed to prefer the small family-owned hotels in the town. Some may also have been encouraged by the resumed practice by competitor hotels, who were up in arms over the decision to build another hotel on the railway site, to send representatives to board the Killarney train at Mallow and to do some direct selling to passengers. Great Southern itself was not immune from the practice. In 1903 a journalist reported seeing 'liveried servants of the Great Southern Hotel' boarding the train at Mallow. Hand bills were distributed announcing the news that the Royal Victoria Hotel was now lighted by electricity, while the Great Southern still relied on gaslight

All of this competition resulted in keen pricing by the Killarney hotels. A Guide published in 1906 describes Killarney, which then had a population of 5,510, as 'a dull uninteresting town', but adds that tourists enjoy good value. 'Prices are not ruinous' it declares, quoting a Great Southern Hotel rate of ten shillings per day for full board and including rail transport from any station served by Great Southern and Western Railways.

Those years were not without their tragedies however. In 1909 a group of waiters from the Great Southern Hotel went swimming in the lake after their day's work. One of their number, Willie Kretzmar, got into difficulties and drowned. He is buried in the New Cemetery in Killarney, commemorated with a gravestone which was erected by staff of the hotel and which bears the following inscription:

Far from his home, no parents near
His friends, so true, watch o'er his bier
They gently laid him here to rest
In the name of those who loved him best.

The new visitors to Killarney had their own ideas of what made a holiday. They included good, wholesome food, nights in the ale house and dancing into the early hours of the morning. The Great Southern directors were once again quick to spot a trend and they decided to build a dance hall on the hotel grounds in 1907.

The East Avenue Hall was fitted with one of the best spring maple floors in Ireland, just the thing for Old Time Waltzes, Polkas and the new craze of jazz. The resident band was the Clarke Barry Orchestra which frequently

Victorian wedding at the Great Southern Hotel

followed an 'all night dance' on a Saturday by giving a recital of sacred music for the more sedate residents of the town on the Sunday afternoon.

Towards the end of the first decade of the 20th Century, the railway, which had revolutionised transportation in Ireland, began to meet with new competition from the motor car and motor coach. The internal combustion engine had made it possible for individuals to acquire their own personal transport, which could bowl along at up to 20 miles per hour and enable the owners to leave, stop and stay wherever they pleased. In the early days, motoring was not for the common man nor indeed for the fainthearted. Road surfaces were still very poor and motor vehicles had a nasty habit of breaking down. They required access to petrol which was not readily available throughout much of the country and was considered to be a danger to both occupants and the general public. Long journeys, say from Dublin to Killarney, were considered to be adventures and the few intrepid motorists who did bring their cars to the Great Southern Hotel were regarded as dashing and daring. Nevertheless the hotel industry had to respond to this new style of visitor and the Great Southern in Killarney decided to convert part of its Post Station for horses into a garage.

The motor coach which emerged around 1910 offered the possibility of carrying larger numbers of visitors, far less than a train of course, but nevertheless significant in terms of bed nights. The railway companies saw the coaches as an immediate and long-term threat to their business and from a very early stage began to invest in coaches and bus companies.

A Tourist Development Company was established in Kerry in 1910 with the assistance of the Great Southern and Western Railway Company which provided a loan of £4,000 for the purchase of motor coaches. The service was further subsidised by Great Southern Hotels on condition that the coaches from Cork would travel via Parknasilla rather than Glengarriff.

These coaches, replicas of which were seen in films like *Ryan's Daughter,* departed Cork at 9am and arrived in Killarney at 7.35pm, depositing their passengers on the doorsteps of the two Great Southern hotels.

This arrangement appeared to be an excellent one for Great Southern, but unfortunately the coaches were frequently delayed and it was not at all unusual for them to stop en-route late in the evening, with passengers staying overnight in a convenient inn or hotel. This pattern did not please Mr Koenig who complained bitterly to the Great Southern Hotels' directors and even offered to pay an additional five per cent on the £350 per year rent of the New Hotel if the coaches could be made to arrive on time.

Other matters bothering the German hotelier included over-booking in the high season and the revived pattern of touting by competitors. In another letter to the Directors in September 1910 he complains that 'I have no room during the season for 450 visitors and as a result I have lost receipts of approximately £225'. His letter urges the Board to build an extension to the New Hotel which would capitalise on the rail link 'as the new motor services are not producing business'.

He was also concerned about renewed attempts by local hotels to take away his business. A letter written in August of that year bitterly complains about 'unchecked touting by a lot of irresponsible hotels and boarding house touts permitted at Mallow Station and on the train and again at Headford Junction and on the Killarney platform. Even on our very doorstep I have seen myself passengers take refuge from this annoyance.'

He attempted to retaliate by getting the Railway to issue combined train and accommodation tickets which would include a room at the New Hotel, but this plan was dropped following objections from other Killarney hoteliers.

Mr Koenig did not get his extension to the New Hotel, but he did get money to create a 'Photographic Dark Room' in the Great Southern Hotel. Photography was the new fashionable hobby and a growing number of hotel guests were arriving with their cameras, tripods, covering sheets, plates and flash guns. They were given to hiring a jarvey to haul themselves and their equipment to the Lakes, Mangerton, the Torc Waterfall or the Gap of Dunloe, where they would painstakingly photograph the scenery. The images recorded on the photosensitive plates could not be seen, however, until the plates were developed and the images printed on photographic paper. This facility was not available to the general public in Killarney and so the Great Southern management decided to provide a dark room for guests where a trained technician helped them develop and print their photographs. The hotel was the first in Ireland to provide such a service.

For those who did not bring a camera to Killarney, an alternative was also available. Louis Anthony, a photographer who was born in Alsace Lorraine in France, had set up shop in the town and provided a service which enabled tourists to take home souvenir photographs of their visit. He employed a team of photographers who cycled each morning to Kate Kearney's Cottage at the Gap of Dunloe, taking with them on their bicycles heavy cameras, tripods and bags of glass photographic plates. They arranged for the tourists to pose for a photograph prior to their departure through the Gap and they then cycled back to Killarney where they developed the plates and printed proof copies. When the tourists arrived at Ross Castle they were shown the proofs and given an opportunity of ordering copies. These orders were processed overnight and the pictures were delivered to customers at their hotels on the following morning. The hotels, including the Great Southern, did not entirely approve of this enterprise and the Anthony photographers were often hindered in their efforts to deliver the prints which had been ordered and to collect their money.

Louis Anthony took many excellent photographs himself in and around Killarney which he published as postcards. These were highly popular with tourists and surviving copies are today prized by collectors.

Among his team of photographers was Daniel MacMonagle who went on to establish a printing business in Killarney and to succeed Louis Anthony as a publisher of postcards. This tradition was further developed by his sons Paddy MacMonagle, the Killarney photographer, writer, folklorist and printer and his brother Sean MacMonagle.

The visitors who departed Killarney with Louis Anthony's souvenir photographs were among the last of the Victorians. Germany was already laying plans for expansion and the inevitable war which would result. As early as 1910 a large number of German spies were placed in Britain and Ireland to undertake an array of tasks including intelligence gathering and mapping. They masqueraded as band masters, teachers and travelling salesmen and helped their country build up an enormous dossier on the two countries.

In August 1912 the Great Southern Hotel received a booking from a gentleman called William Hartman, who was described by the manager as a 'Very Important Person'. This information was conveyed to the front office and housekeeping staff who made special preparations to welcome him. He was allocated Room 25 which was prepared with flowers, a bottle of Port and a blazing coal fire. He was met by the red-uniformed hotel porters at Killarney station and was welcomed to the hotel by Ellen O'Sullivan, a receptionist, who remembered him as 'tall, elegant, handsome and very polite'.

The VIP guest spent the next few days in the hotel, coming and going regularly, taking meals in the restaurant and engaging in games of billiards. Nobody took much notice of him nor did anybody realise that he was in fact a senior German espionage agent called Lodi.

Scotland Yard knew a lot about him, however. They had tracked his activities for several months and were awaiting an opportunity to make an arrest. When news reached them that Lodi was in Ireland and staying at the Great Southern Hotel in Killarney, two detectives were despatched from Scotland Yard armed with an arrest warrant. Under conditions of utmost secrecy they travelled by steamer to Dublin and on to Killarney by train, arriving on the final train of the day at around 11.30pm.

They hastened to the Great Southern Hotel, made themselves known to the manager and went straight to Room 25.

Lodi however had been alerted to their presence and picking up a bulky suitcase of documents, he ran down the back stairs, through the staff quarters and into the boiler room in the basement. In the centre of this room was a very large coal-fired boiler which provided hot water for the entire hotel. The fire under the boiler was burning brightly and Lodi proceeded to open the fire door and throw into the flames sheafs of documents from his suitcase. Before he could burn all of the documents, however, the detectives burst into the boiler room and arrested him. He was taken to Killarney Police Station and held overnight. On the next day he was taken under escort to Dublin by train and from there to the Tower of London. He was subsequently charged, convicted and executed as a spy.

As war clouds gathered over Europe, the British preferred to remain at home. Visitor numbers to Killarney dropped sharply and by 1914 turnover at the Great Southern was down to £6,545 while the New Hotel recorded sales of a mere £1,349.

The Great War had begun and the Victorian Era, during which Killarney had become a resort of international fame, was at an end.

Chapter 8

CHAPTER 8

War and Revolution

The outbreak of the Great War in 1914 had a catastrophic effect on the fledgling Irish tourist industry. Leisure travel between Britain and Ireland came to a standstill, economic activity slowed dramatically and thousands of Irishmen left to fight in the war.

Franz Koenig reported to the Board of the Great Southern Hotels that The New Hotel 'is almost empty' while a local newspaper reported that 'one hundred and sixty people left the Royal Victoria Hotel'. On 6th August the Board gave him permission to close the New Hotel, the East Avenue Hall and the hotels at Caragh Lake and Waterville 'owing to the special conditions prevailing'.

As the 'War to End All Wars' grew in intensity, landed families around Killarney lent what support they could to the troops and Mr Koenig co-operated by opening the fine Coffee Room at the Great Southern Hotel to a Ladies Committee 'interested in a movement for the making of medical requisites for the Military'.

Tourists wait for help beside their broken-down bus near Killarney

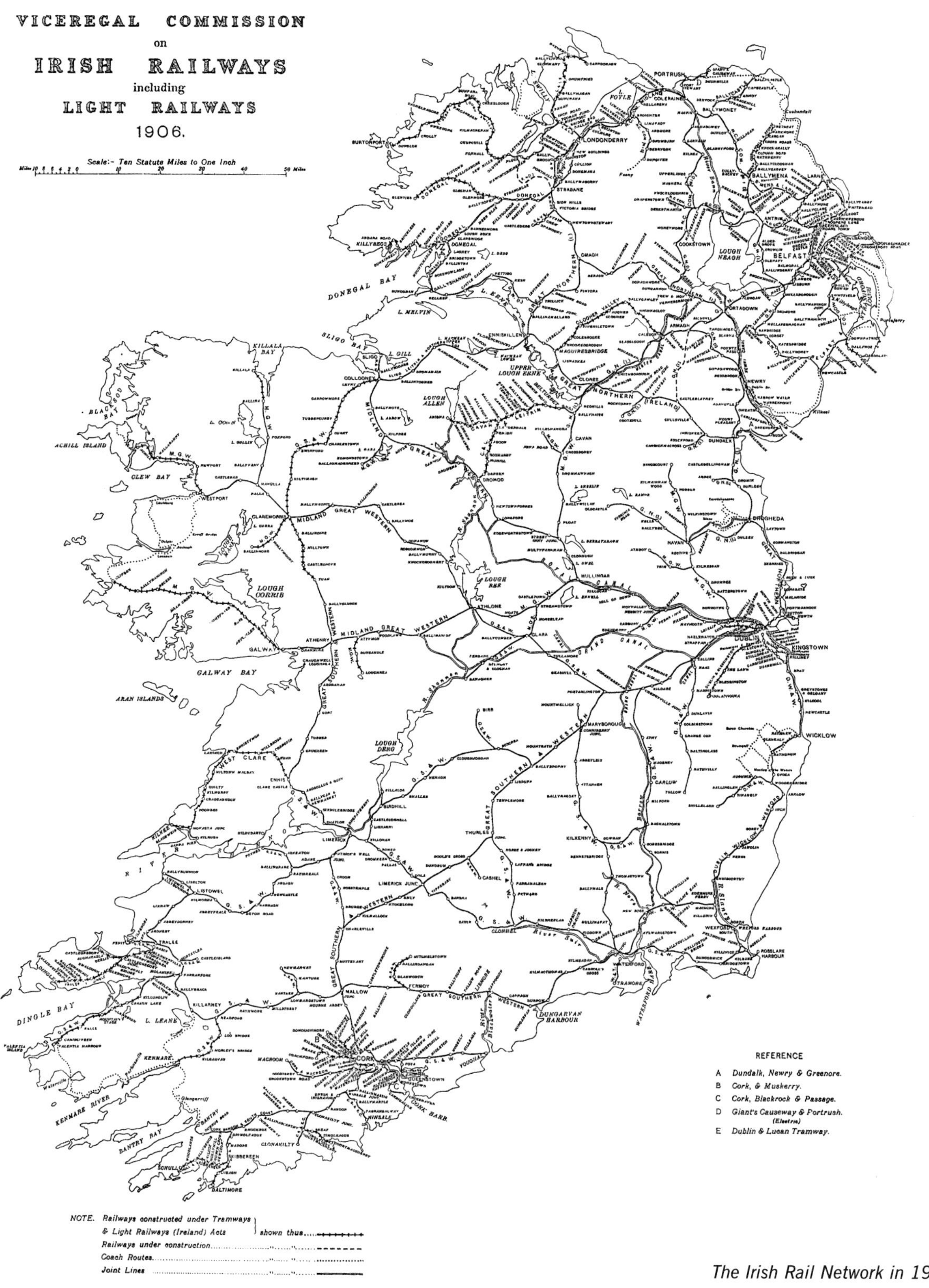

The Irish Rail Network in 1906

These were difficult times for the hotel and its tenant. Some German nationals employed there were interned and while Mr Koenig was allowed continue to operate the hotel, he could not make any money. In June 1915 he told the Directors that he could no longer continue and they agreed to terminate his lease. The Directors decided to take over the operation of the hotel once more and appointed S. J. Medcalf as group hotel manager.

When the new manager arrived in Killarney late in 1915, he was acutely aware that forces other than the Great War were at work. Throughout 1914 the Irish Volunteers had been organising and were openly preparing for a Rebellion. Nowhere was this more evident than in Kerry which had a strong tradition of opposition to British Rule, and nowhere was this opposition made more obvious than at the Oireachtas cultural festival held in Killarney in 1914.

'This was the week that Killarney would never forget', wrote Dorothy McArdle in her book *Kerry's Fighting Story*. 'It was a week of music, song, dance and parades, backgrounded by an industrial exhibition and burnished with the glitter of a great cultural and political resurgence....Puffing trains brought thousands of people into the town and thirty bands from places as far away as Athlone, Dublin, Lusk, Waterford, as well as from the neighbouring counties of Cork and Limerick....Wedged between sidewalks crammed with cheering crowds, hundreds of Volunteers from Killarney and other parts of East Kerry, marched between the bands through decorated streets.'

The Oireachtas was held over a full week, and Dorothy McArdle writes that the third day 'was the most memorable and colourful of all'.

'That was the day that the growing strength and the ardour of the Irish Volunteers first became really obvious in Kerry. From most parts of Kerry as well as from many other parts of the province, including the cities of Limerick and Cork, flocked several thousand Volunteers. The local Company stole most of the thunder of the day as they were the only armed group in the great assemblage. The slouch-hatted Killarney boys had rifles with bayonets atop, jutting out from their shoulders'.

The public were apparently amazed and the local Military more than curious about the origin of these weapons. It turned out that they had been stored in a shed behind the New Hotel and were in fact the property of the Kalem film company which was 'shooting' in the area. The American producers were only too pleased to loan their 'props' to the Volunteers as a means of generating some excitement.

After the Volunteers handed back their uniforms and mock guns to the film company, they continued to drill and train and by early 1916 they were ready to participate in the planned Rebellion. Just prior to the Easter Rising two officers went to Dublin to collect some real arms, including 52 Martini Lee Enfield rifles, which were consigned to Killarney by train as 'cutlery for the Great Southern Hotel'. Needless to say the guns did not arrive in the stores, but were whisked away from the station.

The Rebellion, of course, was eventually confined to Dublin, but shortly afterwards, in May 1916, five of the Killarney Volunteer leaders were arrested and detained in the New Hotel.

Just before their arrest on 17th May 1916, Major N. H. Grimshaw of the Fourth Connaught Rangers arrived at the hotel with an Order for the billeting of his 25 officers and 100 men. There was no shortage of empty rooms in the hotel and the resident manager, A. H. Kirkham, had little difficulty in accommodating his military guests.

A touring party prepares to leave the Great Southern Hotel for the Lakes
(Lawrence Collection, National Library of Ireland)

However, the initial courtesies quickly gave way to a frosty relationship. Major Grimshaw complained several times about the standard of cooking and the quality of service. He also posted a Guard in the lobby of the hotel, which the manager found to be offputting to other guests. He asked the Major why the soldiers on guard should be 'ensconced in the front hall, smoking, reading and sitting on the settees'.

Mr Kirkham reported these matters to his Directors who forwarded a copy to General Friend, the head of military operations in Ireland. The Directors explained the charges which would be levied for accommodating the troops and asked 'if it is necessary for the hall of the hotel in Killarney to be occupied by troops when guests are present'.

The soldiers resident in the New Hotel were not universally popular with the local community and a scuffle broke out between soldiers and locals shortly after their arrival. The locals were arrested and charged with assault and the holder of the hotel's drink licence, a 'Mr Crawford' also found himself before the local Petty Sessions in June 1916 for allowing disorderly conduct at the hotel. He was fined £5, but the Magistrates refrained from endorsing the licence.

Meanwhile the Great Southern was deprived of most of its German-born staff, who were mainly waiters. Following the outbreak of War they were interned, although as we have mentioned Mr Koenig was allowed to continue as lessee and manager. He was certainly there when the German spy Lodi checked into the hotel in 1912 and may have been around in 1915 when the *Lusitania* was sunk by a German U-Boat off the Old Head of Kinsale. Local people told of the presence of a U Boat in Kenmare Bay about a week before the torpedo attack on 7th May, and there are reports that the captain dined with German friends at the Great Southern Hotel in Kenmare.

With business at an all time low the Great Southern and the New Hotel struggled on and the Directors agreed at a meeting in 1917 to install a telephone in the hotel, having been offered the number 'Killarney 26'. The Board also agreed to plant ivy which would eventually cover the walls of the unsightly laundry at the Great Southern. Later that year they also took a decision to keep the Great Southern open during the winter of 1918, but advised the manager to 'work as economically as possible'.

This appears to have been a wise decision for business began to pick up. A total of 7,276 visitors were accommodated at the Great Southern in 1919, producing revenue of £9,517. The following year, 1920, was something of a disaster, however, when visitor numbers fell to 1,652 and revenue to £2,907, but nevertheless the Board spent money on installing a lift from the kitchen to the Coffee Room and Dining Room, much to the relief of waitresses who until then had to carry trays up two flights of 26 steps. The Board was told that a waitress might have to make such a journey ten times while serving a meal to three tables of diners.

In July of that year the Great Southern ceased to be a hotel when it was suddenly taken over by the Military and converted into a barracks. The elegant Coffee Lounge became a general office, bedrooms were packed with army bunks, wines were removed from the cellars and the entire building was fortified. As Maurice O'Leary wrote in 1954:

'Barbed wire defences were thrown up all around the buildings. Plush curtains gave way to sandbags. Sentries with fixed bayonets guarded the approaches and cavalry horses pranced up and down the avenues, along which, in peaceful times, had jogged the horses of the jarveys.'

This event is recorded in the minutes of the Great Southern and Western Railway Company with remarkable brevity. The final item recording proceedings at the meeting on 23rd July 1920 is:

'Mr Medcalf reported that the Killarney Hotel has been occupied by the Military.'

1991 Employee of the Year Timmy Corcoran pictured with P.J. Harnett, Brendan Maher and Deputy General Manager Conor Hennigan

However a meeting of the company's General Purposes Committee held a week later received a letter from Lord Kenmare arising out of a statement by Miss Ryan, then manageress of the Great Southern. She said that staff would be given a fortnight's notice and two weeks pay, but that no further compensation would be paid. Lord Kenmare asked the Board to provide or seek compensation and they passed on his request to the Government. The claim was rejected by the Government on 19th August and the Board then decided to refer the matter to the Defence of the Realm Losses Commission - but again without a successful outcome.

Jarveys at Kate Kearneys Cottage *(Lawrence Collection, National Library of Ireland)*

The Military used the Great Southern as a strategic base, close to the railway, from where it engaged the IRA in the rapidly escalating War of Independence, which had erupted following the execution in Dublin of the Leaders of the 1916 Rising. The hotel was surrounded by armoured vehicles and soldiers kept a close eye on all passengers arriving by train. Nowhere in the country however did the British Army meet with greater resistance than in Kerry and Cork. With Michael Collins directing operations, IRA activity in the area was continuous, well organised and effective and British convoys were repeatedly ambushed.

Intelligence was a key factor in the success of the IRA in Kerry and much of this vital information emanated from the Great Southern and other Killarney hotels. Among the most successful of IRA intelligence agents was John Keogh, who worked as a porter at the International Hotel. Every day his duties would take him to the station to meet the train and he kept his eyes and ears open for useful information. On 2nd March 1921 around 4.25pm, he chatted amiably to a Lieutenant Sherwood while they awaited the arrival of the train. As they did so a number of armoured vehicles sped around the corner and pulled up opposite the steps of the Great Southern Hotel, then a military barracks. 'I must be off now, this is the General', the Lieutenant remarked, and strolled across to join a Major and a General on the steps of the hotel.

John Keogh contacted a friend called Rogers, who was the canteen chef at the hotel and discovered that the high ranking officers would stay at the Great Southern for three days before departing for Buttevant in a blue car. He passed this information to Tommy McEllistrim and Sean Moylan, two prominent members of the local brigade of the IRA and they in turn discovered that the officers were General Cummins and Major Melleney, who were high on the IRA 'hit list'. Their car was duly attacked at Clonbannin in Co. Cork in one of the most famous ambushes of the War of Independence which resulted in the officers being killed and Maurice Slattery, an IRA hostage who was travelling with them, regaining his freedom.

The incident is recalled by John Keogh in *Kerry's Fighting Story*, in which he also tells of 'the only instance of interchange of prisoners' which took place shortly before the Truce. This resulted in a meeting between the Commanding Officer of the military in Killarney and the Brigade OC of the IRA. It resulted in the simultaneous release of a British Major, whose capture John Keogh had brought about and Jack Shanahan, a chemist from Castleisland who was a prisoner in the Great Southern Hotel.

A lull in the fighting encouraged the Directors of Great Southern Hotels to plan a re-opening of the Killarney hotel in 1921, if it was by then vacated by the Military. An indication that matters were improving was the re-opening of the line from Banteer to Tralee in April 1921. It was a 'false dawn' however as the war intensified and the lines were closed again within a month. And to add to their difficulties the Board was faced with a claim from Great Southern Hotel employees for compensation for earnings lost during the military occupation of the hotel. This claim was promptly forwarded to the Government.

Following the Truce both the Great Southern and the New Hotel were taken over by the Irish Republican Army, but once again this occupation was to be brief. Within months a Civil War had broken out between those who supported and opposed a Treaty with the British Government which created a new Irish Free State of 26 Counties with six counties of Northern Ireland remaining within the United Kingdom.

On 11th February 1922 an Order signed by the Officer Commanding Second Kerry Brigade of Óglaigh na hEireann (the Irish Republican Army which opposed the Treaty) provided for the commandeering of the New Hotel 'and certain contents' and announced that the Brigade ' is now entering possession.'

This Order was followed within days with a request from the same OC 'that repairs to the New Hotel be immediately undertaken.'

On 16th February the Directors forwarded a copy of this Order to the Minister for Defence in the Provisional Government, Richard Mulcahy, having first advised him of the occupation by telegram.

The IRA appear to have confined their activities to the New Hotel and by mid-summer had begun to use it as a bomb-making factory. S.J. Medcalf, an unflappable hotel manager, if there ever was one, inspected the hotels and on 25th July wrote the following memo to his superiors:

'I beg to report that the Irregular Forces in possession of the New Hotel at Killarney are manufacturing mines and bombs in the grounds and occasionally discharge them for testing purposes. They have also erected a large shed in the grounds.'

The New Hotel and its grounds proved to be too public a place for bomb-making however and later in 1922 the IRA decided to evacuate the building, as a large force of the Free State Army was on its way to Killarney. Before leaving however they torched the New Hotel, whose embers were still glowing when the Free State soldiers arrived.

An early touring motor coach outside the Great Southern Hotel, Killarney

The Free State Army were the next non-paying guests at the Great Southern. They retained most of the fortification put in place by the British and converted the basement into a prison, fitting iron bars to all the windows and reinforcing doors. Prisoners held there carved their names on the shutters and these remained visible for many years. The Army also converted the handsome Coffee Room into an oratory.

Over the next few months the hotel and its environs were the scene of several skirmishes and raids. A young IRA volunteer called Partalan O'Murchu from Oilean Chiarrai (Castleisland), was shot dead on 19th September 1922. A plaque to his memory was later erected by the National Graves Association and can be seen on the station wall directly opposite the entrance to the Great Southern Hotel.

In her book *Tragedies of Kerry*, Dorothy Macardle tells the story of 'Bertie Murphy', a seventeen-year-old IRA volunteer who was shot dead on the steps of the Great Southern Hotel. He was a captain in the Fianna (IRA) and was captured while on the run. He was taken to the Great Southern Hotel where he was used as a hostage by Free State troops sent to dismantle IRA barricades. According to Dorothy Macardle he was shot in reprisal for an IRA ambush on a Free State patrol, although the authorities at the time claimed that he was shot in an ambush at Brennan's Glen.

Free State officers, a Friar and a Nurse on the steps of the Great Southern Hotel

Prisoners held and interrogated in the basement of the hotel included Jeremiah Donoghue, Stephen Buckley, Daniel Donoghue and Tim Murphy who were killed by the Free State Army at Countess's Bridge near the town on 7th March 1923. In an irony that was typical of the Civil War, both Donoghue and Tadgh Coffey had fought the Black and Tans in the previous year. In the Civil War they found themselves on the side of de Valera and were arrested at Coffey's home in Barleymount on 22nd February 1923. They were taken to the Great Southern Hotel where they were interrogated and charged with possession of arms. They were sentenced to execution and placed in the 'condemned cell' in the basement where they met up with two other prisoners, Stephen Buckley, and Tim Murphy.

An army tailor called Sugrue, who was working in the barracks brought them bottles of stout and wished them well. He had heard the soldiers upstairs selecting a firing squad to carry out the executions. On the following morning Sugrue had better news - they were to be reprieved. The reprieve did not last, however. On 7th March the prisoners were taken to a field at Countess's Bridge where bombs were exploded. Three of the prisoners died, but Tighe Coffey miraculously survived and succeeded in reaching the home of a friend and comrade, Jack Moynihan in Kilcummin.

In a day of great tragedy nine Republican prisoners were also blown up by the Free State Army at Ballyseedy Cross near Tralee.

And some time later the tailor Sugrue was shot dead by Free State Troops when he returned one evening to barracks at the Great Southern Hotel.

Chapter 9

CHAPTER 9

Rebirth

Wars end, even World Wars, Wars of Independence and Civil Wars and eventually life edges back towards normality.

So it was at Great Southern Hotels in 1924. Once the Free State Army had left, S.J. Medcalf sent a team of managers to inspect the Killarney hotels. There was not very much to inspect at the New Hotel which had been burned to the ground and was clearly beyond repair. The Great Southern had, however, remained more or less intact apart from damage to interior walls, windows, doors, bedrooms and the kitchen. The basement had been turned into a jail and the managers found beds there which they described as 'filthy'.

The objectives of Great Southern were to get back into business as quickly as possible and to be compensated for the damage caused to its property. Even before the Free State Army occupation, the Directors had made a claim on the British War Office for £4,788 0s 8d in respect of damage caused to the two hotels. This included £519 1s 8d for furniture and £1,297 3s 3d for painting and paper.

The claim on the Free State Government was however much larger. Great Southern claimed a total of £18,3864s2d in respect of 'the malicious destruction of the New Hotel and its contents'.

That claim was lodged in 1924 after the Great Southern Hotel had been handed back by the Free State Army. The Dublin auctioneer and valuer James Adam was asked to 'assess the deficiencies and damages caused by military occupation' and was urged to report as quickly as possible. By June he had completed his work and accompanied a Great Southern director and S.J. Medcalf on a deputation to the Minister for Industry and Commerce which resulted in the company getting an assurance that its compensation claim would be met sympathetically. In fact the claim was settled in the following year for £10,750. Great Southern had earlier received £2,320 from the British Government.

While damage was being assessed by James Adam, work was progressing on refurbishing the hotel. New furniture and bedding , including 'hair mattresses, feather bolsters, pillows and white satin quilts' were ordered from London, carpets were being made specially in Cork and the hotel's cutlery, crockery and other equipment, which had been put into storage, was taken out and polished. In a remarkable operation the hotel was redecorated and was back in business by June 1924 - a mere six months after the army had left. The East Avenue Hall was painted and re-opened and the final bill for the work came to £6,000.

The fate of 'the New Hotel' had been sealed, however, and it was finally demolished in 1925. The Directors had debated the idea of rebuilding the hotel from the ground up, but decided instead to invest the compensation money in the Great Southern and in a new Refreshment Room which would be built alongside the Railway Station. This new premises had a dining room with 120 covers and its own kitchen. The original estimate for the building was £7,940, but on this occasion the actual cost worked out significantly lower at £5,579.

As the hotel was being restored, the hotel management was also taking steps to win back business. A small space in the grounds was leased to Thomas Cook and Sons at five shillings per year for a Tourist Information

An artist's impression of the Great Southern Hotel

Kiosk where travel tickets were also sold. Efforts were made to renew cruises on the Lakes of Killarney and to revive the 'Great Southern Navy', but many of the boats had been damaged and three, the 'Brenda', 'Florrie' and a Ferry Boat, had simply disappeared. Nevertheless work began on making the other boats - the 'Maureen', 'Cuckoo', 'Alice', 'Jenny', 'Dolly' and 'Killarney' lake-worthy again and by 1925 the Fleet and its Navy were once again sailing on the Lakes.

A new Tourist Coach Service was also launched in 1925 serving Bantry, Glengarriff and Killarney. It was operated by John Wharton who was given a subsidy of £200 towards his costs for the season.

The Board of Great Southern Hotels was more than pleased with the progress achieved and decided that the Directors should travel down to Killarney, experience the pleasures of the Great Southern Hotel and report back.

The Deputy Chairman took up the suggestion and during a weekend at the hotel, he engaged in several games of billiards, playing on the hotel's 'professional' table which was among the finest in the country at the time. It was placed in the centre of the Billiard Room (in an area now occupied by the bar) and its considerable weight was supported by four stone pillars built underneath the floor and extending to the basement where they remain today. The Deputy Chairman was not impressed, however. He reported to the Board that 'New billiard balls are badly needed - as well as some cues'. He also observed that 'People in Killarney do not dance, but I am told that the wireless, when it was there, was very popular.'

The wireless in question had apparently been moved to the Great Southern Hotel in Parknasilla.

The Deputy Chairman reported that 'passengers are molested by the jarveys' at Killarney station and suggested that 'the field behind the hotel, now set with potatoes, should be set with grass.'

Three other directors, Major Henry, Sir James Forde and Mr Goodbody subsequently visited Killarney and reported back to the Board that 'the construction of the (Great Southern) hotel makes it impossible to provide bathrooms attached to bedrooms without taking up other bedrooms of considerable letting value.' The Board agreed and decided instead to increase the number of bathrooms in the hotel from six to nineteen.

The three visiting directors also suggested that Great Southern Hotels 'should get control of another hotel or a house with a good situation near the Lakes and equip it to suit wealthy Americans and other visitors who are prepared to pay a high tariff.' They also suggested converting the Billiard Room into a Writing Room and selling off the billiard table (an idea that surely found little favour with the Deputy Chairman) and replacing a drawing room with three bedrooms. Finally they recommended that the Board should consider 'putting a number of motor boats on the Lakes' - an idea which did not come to fruition until the 1990s when Lake Cruisers were introduced by a latter day pioneering Killarney hotelier, Maurice O'Donoghue.

After much deliberation the Board decided to retain the Billiard Room and even to buy a few new balls and cues. The other suggestions were shelved, but they did agree to spend around £4,000 on improving the hotel's plumbing and drainage.

If these investments were undertaken in anticipation of an improvement in business, the Directors were sadly mistaken. The years to the end of the twenties and into the thirties were truly miserable for business of all kind in Ireland. The Government, under Eamon de Valera became embroiled with the British Government on the issue of paying Land Annuities, and moved rapidly towards an isolationist policy. 'Burn everything British except its coal' became the war cry. High tariffs were imposed on all imports from Britain making it expensive and difficult to secure supplies of essential items for the operation of a hotel such as cutlery, crockery and furnishings. The Government sought to compensate by encouraging new Irish industries, but the goods produced by these fledgling manufacturers were often shoddy. Food, however, was in most plentiful supply and was very cheap because Irish agricultural produce could no longer be exported to Britain. The idea of exporting to Europe at the time was far beyond anyone's imagination.

The Great Southern Hotel therefore had a plentiful supply of cheap food and cheap labour - but precious few paying guests. The Economic War had not only depressed the Irish economy, inflicting further hardship on a population ravaged by more than a decade of war, but it also created a hostile environment in Britain and probably served to deter even those brave people who may have contemplated a visit to Ireland.

The management of the Great Southern managed to keep the hotel open during these difficult days, although it recorded heavy financial losses. Costs were kept to a minimum and revenue was generated from any likely source. The East Avenue Hall, which had been built to accommodate dances and banquets, was leased as a 'picture house' to Thomas G. Cooper, a pioneering impressario who had made a film called *The Dawn*, about the IRA and who introduced the 'Talkies' to Killarney. Only three weeks after he acquired the lease, the timber-framed East Avenue Hall was burned to the ground when a fire broke out after a matinee screening of *The King of Jazz*. Paddy MacMonagle, who was present at the conflagration, during a lunch break from school, recalls that the projectionist, 'Sacky' Cronin, who doubled as a local postman had 'a habit of smoking while working'. It has been speculated that a spark ignited the highly flammable film and the wooden structure of the building which then gloried under the name of 'The Casino Cinema'.

Surprisingly a new hotel, 'The Ross' opened in Killarney in 1933 and proved to be the last of an era. The town had to wait until 1959 before another new hotel opened its doors. It did however receive a priceless gift in 1932 when Bourne Vincent, the owner of the Herbert Estate, donated 1,100 acres of scenic parkland around the Lakes to the State, thereby creating Bourne Vincent Park which is now the central element in Killarney National Park.

President Eamon de Valera inspects a Guard of Honour outside the Great Southern Hotel

Every hotel in Ireland suffered greatly at this time and their plight led to the establishment of the Irish Hotels Federation in 1937. The Federation was formed to protest against the Shop Assistants Bill which was designed to end the exploitation of shop assistants by defining their working hours and minimum levels of pay. The Bill, as originally drafted, extended to hotel workers and took no account of the need of hotels to operate around the clock.

The publication of the Bill prompted hoteliers to ask the age-old question: 'What are we going to do?' which prompted the equally predictable answer: 'Form an Association'. In due course the Irish Hotels Federation was established at a meeting in Dublin on October 28th 1937 and elected J. W. 'Josie' Mongan, a Galwayman and member of the Dáil, as its first president. Great Southern Hotels was among the inaugural members of the Federation and the Killarney hotel paid a first year membership fee of a guinea (approx. 90 cents) which was the highest in the scale and applied only to hotels with 12 rooms or more.

The newly formed Irish Hotels Federation was also aware of moves to promote Irish tourism in an organised manner through the formation of an Irish Tourist Association. This was not a new idea. Indeed a body of the same name was established and registered under the Charitable Societies Act back in 1893 by F. W. Crossley who was manager in Ireland for Thomas Cook and Son Ltd. His original idea was to convince his employers to invest in the promotion of Ireland overseas, but when he met with a lukewarm response, he decided to resign his post and establish the ITA as a private company.

The award-winning gardens at the Great Southern Hotel

He took a keen interest in the emerging railways and published a pamphlet in which he suggested an amalgamation of the railways along the lines of the present Iarnród Eireann. In 1896 Crossley established a company called Development Syndicate (Ireland) Ltd, which acquired a licence to operate a postal service. This company in turn set up the first Shannon Development Company which ran a steamboat service on the River Shannon from 1897. Among the first passengers on the service was the Duke of York , whose top hat Mr Crossley dislodged by accidentally kicking it with his boot as His Highness ascended the gangplank below where he was sitting. The Duke enjoyed his river cruise, however, and Crossley immediately promoted his service as 'The Duke of York Route'.

Shannon Development Company formed an alliance with the railways which ran excursion trains to link with the river cruises and it also built two hotels, the Golfers Hotel at Sutton Cross in Dublin and the Lakeside Hotel, Killaloe. It later bought the Charlemont Hotel in Howth and the Royal Mail Hotel in Dún Laoghaire.

F.W. Crossley was the first entrepreneur to market Ireland as a holiday destination, using techniques like advertising, marketing and public relations. In 1899 he invited a group of British parliamentarians to tour the country, accompanied by several Fleet Street journalists. He was instrumental in establishing the first Hotel and Restaurant Proprietors Association in the country and he set up an Irish Tourism office in London in 1909. This office promoted his burgeoning business, which alas, came to a sudden end with the outbreak of the Great War.

That war and the subsequent Rising and War of Independence in Ireland interrupted the development of tourism, but as the new Irish state emerged, so did the idea of tourism as an industry which could play a vital role in the development of a fledgling Irish economy.

With the Great War behind them, people were beginning to travel again and large ocean liners were arriving almost daily at Southampton carrying visitors from America. If so many Americans were attracted to Britain, then why not to Ireland also?

In his autobiography Christopher S. (Todd) Andrews recalls that following his release from internment in 1924 at the age of 22, he applied for a job with the newly formed Irish Tourism Association (a body which was not in any way connected to F. W. Crossley's company). The ITA operated from a two-room basement office at Westland Row. It had been established a year before by J. C. Foley, who had earlier established the Tourist Organisation Society which merged with the West of Ireland Tourist Development Association in 1924. Todd Andrews recalls that he met some familiar faces at the ITA offices, including J. P. O'Brien, from Ballyporeen, who was a fellow internee at The Curragh, David Barry from Cork and Sean Fitzpatrick from Tipperary, all of whom had been active in the War of Independence.

The ITA was established with the aim of 'promoting tourism to the benefit of the nation', and it operated without any support from the new Irish Free State. Instead it sought funding from the stakeholders in tourism including the railways, shipping lines, hoteliers and retailers. It was also supported by some local Councils and Corporations. By 1926 the ITA had an annual income of £10,000 which it spent largely on producing brochures and guide books as well as a magazine called *Irish Tourism*, which was distributed to travel agents, carriers and tourism promoters at home and abroad.

J. P. O'Brien and his colleagues toured the country, canvassing subscriptions for the ITA. In return they promised hotels an entry in a new *Tourist Guide to Ireland* and the 300 hotels listed in that first Guide, including the Great Southern hotels, constituted the first data base of Irish accommodation which was to be built upon in years to come.

It soon became obvious that the ITA could not effectively promote Ireland as a destination without State support. J. P. O'Brien lobbied successive Governments, but had to wait until 1939 when the Tourist Traffic Act, introduced by the then Minister for Industry and Commerce, Sean Lemass, provided for the establishment of Bord Cuartaíochta na hEireann or the Irish Tourist Board, of which J. P. O'Brien was appointed chairman. The role of the Irish Tourist Association was changed following the Act to concentrate on local tourism promotion and the provision of information through local Tourist Offices, not unlike the service provided by regional Tourism Organisations today. The ITA was given a seat on the new Irish Tourist Board and it also received an annual grant from the state body.

The Tourist Traffic Act of 1939 also obliged all hotels to register with the new Irish Tourist Board and those who did not comply were obliged to remove from their premises any sign bearing the word 'Hotel'. Great Southern Hotel, Killarney was among the first to register with the ITB and it was only then, 85 years after its opening that the 'Grand Old Lady of Killarney' became 'officially recognised' as a hotel.

The new Irish Tourist Board acquired offices at 13 Merrion Square, but no sooner did it recruit its first staff than war again broke out in Europe and all thoughts of tourism were abandoned for the next six years.

The Irish Hotels Federation, meanwhile, had been unsuccessful in its attempts to gain exemption for hotel workers from the provisions of the Shops Act and a Mrs Fawcett of Seaview Hotel, Ballycotton was successfully sued for non-payment of overtime to an employee. But the IHF finally prevailed and in 1941 the Act was amended to exclude hotel workers.

As hoteliers from around the country considered these issues at their annual meeting in 1939, however, their agenda was overshadowed by a momentous event - the outbreak of World War Two.

In every nation of the world, this catastrophic episode in human history is remembered as The War. In Ireland, however, it was called the National Emergency. This country remained neutral in the conflict between the Allies and Hitler's Germany and the danger to hotels therefore, came not from bombs, but from shortages of soap, whiskey and other essentials of life. Shortly after the outbreak of the war, food rationing was introduced and hotels began a five-year long battle with the Government for preferential supplies and extra rations. The Civil Servants were not very accommodating, however, and politicians took the view that at a time such as this, the citizens of a neutral country should abstain from travel and entertainment. There was also a suspicion that if hotels were given unrestricted access to scarce food supplies, wealthy customers might dine in hotels regularly as a means of circumventing the general rationing - and this would be neither popular nor politically correct. Hotels nevertheless had to survive and were conscious of the threat which the War presented to the jobs of their employees. Hoteliers and their managers therefore used every possible strategy to fill their larders and cellars, often travelling every by-road of the country on 'black market' buying trips. It comes as no surprise that records of the Great Southern Hotel over the period carry no references to these buying excursions, but if the managers of the day did not buy regularly on the black market, they would have been unique in the industry.

The cost of stocking the hotel rose sharply during the war years and this is reflected in an increase of 15 per cent in the daily rate in 1942 and a similar increase in the following year.

killarney Police Barracks

Those hotels which were lucky enough to secure supplies of beers, wines and spirits were faced with a threat to their sale to guests during the early years of the War. A new Intoxicating Liquor Bill provided drinking opportunities to 'bona fide' travellers, but would have prohibited guests from buying alcohol after 11pm and would also have barred hotels from serving drink to residents on Christmas Day and St Patrick's Day. The Irish Hotels Federation lobbied against these proposals which were eventually dropped.

The war years were not a total disaster for the Great Southern hotel, however. Those Irish families who could afford to do so spent time in Kerry and the commercial business did not fully dry up. The hotel was also frequented by members of the legal profession visiting the town and they were often joined by American GIs based in Northern Ireland who travelled south during their leave periods bringing with them American cigarettes and nylon stockings, which made them hugely popular with local girls.

After the Allies landed on the beaches of Normandy in 1944, an early end of the conflict became likely and the Great Southern Hotel, Killarney, like the country's tourism leaders, began to gird themselves for an expected post-war boom.

It would happen alright - but would lead to more dark days.

Chapter 10

CHAPTER 10

A New Owner

The immediate aftermath of the War brought a massive influx of visitors to Ireland, principally from Britain where food shortages still prevailed. Even before then, the Irish Tourist Board began to recruit staff and set about preparing a new *Guide to Hotels and Guest Houses*. The invitation to apply for inclusion in this Guide received a massive response from publicans, boarding house owners and hoteliers, who were acutely aware that if they did not register with the ITB, they would be obliged to remove 'Hotel' signs from their premises. When the Guide was published in 1945 therefore it listed 1,200 'hotels', many of which were actually pubs or boarding houses. The great value of that Guide was that it provided the ITB with a list of premises which could subsequently be checked and graded. The Board appointed Fintan Lawlor, a maths teacher at Synge Street, as its first inspector and advertised for other inspection staff. It received 1,800 applications, a measure of the attraction of the job and the acute unemployment which existed in Ireland at the time, and the successful candidates were Donal O'Sullivan, an Irish chess champion, who became senior inspector, Kevin Durnin, who had travelled extensively in Europe, Kitty Kennedy, a domestic science teacher, and Seaghan O'Briain, a founder member of An Óige and a strong supporter of the Irish language movement.

This intrepid team of inspectors set about visiting each of the 1,200 registered hotels, travelling by bicycle, on foot, on trains which frequently broke down and eventually in one of two ancient Ford cars acquired by the ITB. The inspections were basic by the standards of today. The hotels visited were suffering from shortages of basic maintenance products like paint and timber as well as fuel for boilers and plumbing fittings. The ITB took a strong line with those premises who refused to register and many were prosecuted and fined for failing to remove their 'Hotel' signs.

The inspectors concentrated on advising on hygiene standards. After each visit a report was written and these reports, while basic, became invaluable when the Board decided to introduce grading in 1946. This exercise involved the Inspectors again visiting all registered premises and placing them in a Grade on the basis of their facilities and services. Great Southern Hotel, Killarney, received an 'A' grading, the highest available and reserved for 'luxury hotels of the highest quality'.

Meanwhile tourism in Ireland was booming, with the British market particularly buoyant. Thousands of visitors came from across the Irish Sea to sample our food and drink and tour our scenic areas including Killarney. They were given a 'Céad Míle Fáilte' everywhere they went and it was during this period that the goodwill of the British visitor was won. Indeed memories of post-war holiday experiences in Ireland were to remain with British visitors for more than two decades.

Meanwhile rapid changes were taking place in the transport industry. The railways, which had been the principal carrier of visitors to Killarney for nine decades, were meeting with new competition from motor cars and coaches. Henry Ford, with his assembly line system of car building, which was carried out at plants like Dagenham in England and Cork, had put private motoring within the means of thousands of ordinary people while the buses, which emerged from similar assembly lines, were carrying groups of 15 to 30 people at a time over a much improved road network. Getting into the bus business was relatively easy and inexpensive and literally hundreds of entrepreneurs launched local services using small Bedford buses which could accommodate 14 to 16 passengers. The buses also had the advantage over the railways that they could travel wherever even a rudimentary road existed and they often provided a 'feeder' service linking a railway station like Killarney with a hotel in Caragh Lake or Parknasilla. Private car ownership was also booming with the number of cars registered in the country soaring from 9,246 in 1923 to 48,599 by 1938.

Lumbered with massive overheads such as the maintenance of railway track, stations and rolling stock and a workforce which was well organised in trade unions and therefore enjoyed good pay and conditions, the great railway companies of Ireland plunged into losses and debt during the twenties and thirties. As early as 1923 the Great Southern and Western Railway Company threatened to cease operations because of 'acute financial difficulties'. The fledgling Free State Government stepped in with financial support, which was the first State subsidy of the railways. It also established a Railways Commission to examine the viability of the network which, in its report, advocated State ownership of the entire railway system. The Government disagreed arguing that the system could become self-financing if the various railway companies amalgamated. Early in 1923 it warned that if the railways did not voluntarily amalgamate by July of that year, they would be compulsorily acquired. Owned by a wide range of shareholders and various Board of Directors, each with its own agenda, the railways talked about amalgamation, but allowed the Government deadline to pass. A Bill to force amalgamation was published in the following year and this produced some results with Great Southern and Western Railways merging with the Midland Great Western Railway to create Great Southern Railways.

Amalgamation however did not solve the strategic problems of the railways and Great Southern continued to lose money. The Government pressed ahead with its plans to rationalise the railway system, and, after a Bill to achieve this was defeated in 1944, it was forced to call a General Election. The Fianna Fáil Government was re-elected and it immediately revived the legislation which created a new company to own all the railways in the Free State. It was called Córas Iompair Éireann and, when it came into being on New Year's Day 1945, Great Southern Hotels changed ownership for only the second time in its history.

In its original form, CIE was a private enterprise company which, in addition to six Great Southern Hotels, acquired 2,000 miles of rail track, 500 locomotives, 800 carriages, 1,300 freight wagons, 600 buses, 500 road freight vehicles, 300 horses, 40 trams and one Royal Canal.

The new company tried valiantly to absorb its various businesses, but endured a major setback in the winter of 1947 which was one of the most severe on record both in Ireland and in Britain. Snow drifts, gales and blizzards made it impossible to mine and transport the coal which was vital to keep the locomotives running and the hotel fires burning. Trains were cancelled, buses were confined to their garages and the Great Southern Hotel in Killarney was virtually empty. In that one year CIE recorded a massive loss of £900,000, which proved to be crippling. It struggled on for another two years, but was finally nationalised in 1950, when, after 96 years of private ownership, Great Southern Hotel, Killarney became the property of the Government of the recently created Republic of Ireland.

The early days of the new State transport company were not without controversy, with much media interest in a report which revealed that in its most difficult days the Board of Great Southern Railways had considered investing the then enormous sum of £1m in a new luxury hotel to be built at Glengarriff where it had earlier acquired the old Roches Hotel and a piece of prime building land. The project was, however, abandoned by the Board before the company was nationalised.

In their very first report, the Directors of the new CIE said that the Great Southern Hotels were operating successfully 'and money and care are being expended to ensure that they are being maintained in a first class condition'. This report also reveals that for a period in the late 1940s a contract was awarded to a company called Gordon Hotels to manage all of the Great Southern Hotels, dining on the railway cars and the station refreshment rooms and buffets. This contract was not renewed by CIE. The new Board also decided to close the hotels at Mulrany and Parknasilla during the winter months and to reduce staff at the Great Southern in Killarney 'to the minimum necessary to meet the amount of business offering during the winter months.' These strategies appeared to work. Great Southern Hotels made a profit of £7,000 during the difficult year of 1950 and profits continued to rise each year, reaching £40,288 in 1958.

These annual reports of CIE also go into considerable detail about the operation of the hotels. The 1952 report says that 'at the Killarney hotel a new souvenir shop was set up for dealing in hand-made products. This has proved very attractive and has been favourably commented on by visitors', while in the following year's report, we learn that 'telephones were installed in a number of bedrooms in each of the Board's six hotels and larger switchboards were installed at Killarney and Parknasilla.' The report for 1956 tells us that 'at the Killarney hotel five additional *en suite* bathrooms were provided bringing the number of private bathrooms in this hotel to twenty-seven. Other improvements in the hotel included a ladies powder room, staff quarters, a kitchen service area and the provision of a mobile cocktail bar for use at functions and dances.'

In 1957 the company reported a far more substantial development at Killarney Great Southern - the construction of a new wing, known as The Link Corridor, of thirty-three *en suite* bedrooms.

Teresa Keogh joined the staff of Great Southern Hotel, Killarney two years before the hotel was nationalised. 'I lived just across the road and from a very young age I dreamed of working there. I saw the porters in their bright red uniforms and the visitors passing through the elegant front door', she recalls.

She was taken on as a trainee waitress and for the next twenty years she 'enjoyed every minute of working there'.

Despite the economic difficulties of the country and the financial crisis faced by the hotel's owners, Teresa remembers the Great Southern as an elegant place.

'The dining room had a formal atmosphere with the waiters dressed in tails. For banquets and special occasions we also wore white gloves. I had a black uniform and white starched apron which I carefully laundered every evening. The pleats at the back of the apron had to be perfectly straight. The waiting staff would be inspected by the Head Waiter, but we had great pride in our work and in our appearance, so it was most unusual for anything to be amiss.'

She made life-long friends from among her colleagues including chambermaids who carried large jugs of hot water up three flights of stairs to the guest rooms, porters who ferried buckets of coal and kept the fires burning, chefs who toiled in the hot, poorly ventilated kitchen and page boys who ran errands and operated the lifts.

Above all, she remembers the exceptionally high standards maintained by a succession of female general managers, including the 'tall and precise' Miss Curvin who was in charge when Teresa arrived in 1948, and Miss Noreen O'Rourke and Miss Elizabeth McCarthy who succeeded her.

The guests who stayed at the Great Southern in the early fifties were wealthy English tourists and wealthy Irish families. They frequently arrived at the front door in chauffeur-driven Rolls-Royce and Bentley motor cars which were carefully parked during their stay in one of the hotel's garages located near the Franciscan Friary. The relationship between the Friars and the hotel has always been close and cordial. The Friary itself was built around the time that the Railway Hotel opened and staff who lived in the hotel regularly attended the 6.30am

Mass there for more than 100 years. The only discordant note was sounded in the 1880s when hotel guests objected to being woken by the 6am Angelus bell and the Good Friars somewhat reluctantly agreed to postpone the first Angelus of the day until noon.

Guests of the Great Southern in the fifties tended to like their food and would regularly partake of a full 'Irish' breakfast, morning coffee, four course lunch, afternoon tea, five course dinner and a midnight snack. The charges included 12s.6d (66c) for dinner, 7s.6d (31c) for lunch while a room with breakfast cost £1. 0s. 8d (€1.30).

Throughout these meals they were served by one of the most professional teams ever to grace an Irish hotel, who not only provided a Silver Service, but could also prepare flambés, a Steak Tartare or Crêpes Suzette. It included head waiter Jimmy Cullinane, a Dubliner, who had first visited Killarney when he worked on the train dining cars and who gave 47 years of loyal service to the hotel, sommelier Paddy Sheridan, who was guaranteed to 'keep the party going', Timmy O'Connor, Tommy Regan and the present Maitre D, Richard Whelan.

Josie Mongan, founder of the Irish Hotels Federation with Canon Heany and Cardinal McRory in the gardens of the Carna Hotel

Also a Dubliner, Richard followed in the steps of Jimmy Cullinane by working on the railway dining cars from the age of 15. He too was captivated by the romanticism of the great railway hotels and worked initially at the Sligo Great Southern before moving to Killarney in 1955.

He recalls the halcyon days of the fifties when chauffeurs would gather in the evenings in the Stewards' Room which was located in an area now occupied by Peppers restaurant. He dined at the Great Southern too every day, around the large table in the basement, where staff meals were served and the gossip of the day was exchanged. And he was a permanent resident for many years, sleeping in one of a dozen staff bedrooms also located in the basement, indeed in the very area which served as a prison cell while the hotel was occupied by the Free State Army in the twenties.

'Local staff lived at home, but Dubs like me, lived in', says Richard, adding 'men on one side of the house and women on the other.'

But he does not pretend that it was an easy life. 'One man would be up at 4.30am to start the huge coal range in the kitchen. From 6.30 am the chefs and waiters would be on duty. It was a noisy, busy, hot place with much shouting and clattering of pots and pans. The chefs worked around a central stove, producing hundreds of dishes every day. We worked up to sixteen hours a day, six and half days a week, before the hotel was unionised. Then we got a full day off every week.'

Jackie O'Sullivan, a director of Great Southern Hotels and former head barman at Killarney, who joined the hotel in 1957, also remembers long hours 'and service of an unbelievable standard'. 'Every bedroom had a bell and within seconds of it being rung by a guest a member of staff would be on hand to provide whatever service was needed. Each floor had four house girls constantly on duty, just to respond to those bells.'

Few rooms were en-suite and guests bathed in one of the seventeen bathrooms. P.J. Hartnett, a former head porter, recalls that the bathrooms were in constant use and had to be thoroughly cleaned and the bath disinfected after each guest.

Passengers arriving by train would be met by the porters who included Jack and Tim Moriarty and Paddy McCarthy, who collected luggage and led their guests down a covered walkway close to the station wall and across the cobbled street to the hotel door. When VIPs like President Sean T. O'Ceallaigh, Taoiseach Eamon de Valera or even Queen Salote of Tonga arrived (and she did in 1952), a red carpet was laid along the walkway stretching up the steps to the front door of the hotel. In the case of the six foot monarch however the hotel management also borrowed a Victorian four poster bed capable of supporting her twenty-stone weight (280lbs/127kg). Other visitors to get the 'red carpet treatment' included Cardinal Spelman of New York, Walt Disney and the 'New York Cosmetic Queen', Peggy Sage.

The red carpet was laid many times in 1954 when Great Southern Hotel Killarney celebrated its centenary with a series of special dinners.

The centenary was celebrated in a difficult economic climate. The post-war boom had dissipated and the numbers of tourists visiting Ireland in general and Killarney in particular, had fallen. The Government response was to establish two new organisations, An Bord Fáilte and Fógra Fáilte which had responsibility for the development of tourism and its promotion. The experiment had only limited success, principally because of poor communications between Bord Fáilte, the development body and Fógra Fáilte, the promotional organisation. A change of Government was followed by the amalgamation of the two organisations into Bord Fáilte Eireann, under the Tourist Traffic Act of 1955.

Both An Bord Fáilte and Fógra Fáilte did, however, take some long-lasting initiatives during their short lives as individual organisations. *Ireland of the Welcomes*, a magazine designed to project a positive image of Ireland, was launched in 1952. Its editor for 17 years was Michael Gorman, who engaged the best writers, illustrators and photographers available in the country to produce a high quality publication which attracted 10,000 subscribers in its first year, a figure which was to rise to 120,000 during the eighties.

The first acting director general of BFE was Dr Gerry Dempsey, who took on the task of integrating the staffs and cultures of the two former tourism bodies. He commissioned a report from Urwick Orr and Partners which advocated a structure in which managers would have a high level of personal responsibility. This policy was implemented with enthusiasm and considerable flair by BFE's first full-time director general, Dr Timothy O'Driscoll, who was appointed in 1956. A former civil servant, he had served in the Aviation Section of the Department of Industry and Commerce when new airports were being built at Shannon and Dublin. Later he became chief executive of Coras Tráchtála, the Irish Export Board before moving to Canada as head of the

International Air Travel Association (IATA). From there he moved back to the Department of External Affairs and became, for a time, Irish Ambassador to the Netherlands.

He made an immediate impact on Bord Fáilte, encouraging an entrepreneurial culture among managers and linking up with his former colleague, Kevin Barry, who had helped design the new airports at Collinstown (Dublin) and Shannon and was now in charge of hotel and product development at Bord Fáilte. To this work, Tim O'Driscoll added the activity of marketing. Funds were obtained under Marshall Aid to finance a study of the industry, and Bord Fáilte began to segment markets, to aim at groups of people likely to visit Ireland and to establish contacts with the travel trade in America and other overseas markets.

Parallel with this marketing activity, Bord Fáilte sought to encourage the development of the accommodation sector with a package of grants and incentives. Initially the industry was slow to respond during a period of economic stagnation, and it was not until Intercontinental Hotels was attracted to build three new hotels at Dublin, Cork and Limerick in 1956, that other hoteliers began to avail of the Bord Fáilte incentive package. The 'carrots' available at the time included a State Guaranteed Loan Scheme offering loans at 3.75% interest and a grant of £275 towards the cost of a new hotel double bedroom with bath.

Denis Collins, head porter, wishes Mr T.F. O'Higgins well during his presidential campaign

As the number of hotel bedrooms grew, Bord Fáilte stepped up its marketing campaigns, particularly in America. Groups of travel writers were brought to Ireland where they sampled the product and major promotions were staged at the annual conference of the American Society of Travel Agents (ASTA) where the flair and innovative approach of the Irish compensated for the relatively small budgets available. As a result, close bonds were established with key members of the American travel trade. Bord Fáilte also made good use of TV and radio, with Tim O'Driscoll proving to be an accomplished performer. These campaigns proved to be highly successful and sustained our tourism industry during a time of deep economic recession.

In 1953 Bord Fáilte was the instigator of a novel project which was to lift the spirits of the entire population. 'An Tóstal' was a new Spring Festival designed to encourage national progress in every field of endeavour, extend the tourist season, encourage civic spirit and national pride and give every city, town and village an opportunity to celebrate. Tóstal Committees were set up in 52 cities, towns and villages and each was invited to devise a programme of carnival and cultural events. A special An Tóstal Flag was designed and was

Charlie Chaplin with his daughters and his wife Oonagh at the Great Southern Hotel Killarney. (Denis Collins is at the back on the left)

ceremonially raised at the beginning of the festival. The inaugural An Tóstal was a great success as the population, depressed by unemployment and emigration, seized on the opportunity to celebrate. The Great Southern Hotel Killarney joined in the spirit of the festival by holding a series of special dinners and dances. There were parades, carnivals, parties, bunting and some high jinks in many places, including Dublin where an ornamental sculpture which had been placed on O'Connell Bridge was dumped into the Liffey.

An Tóstal continued for the next five years and its success was best measured in the manner in which it revived celebration in Ireland rather than the number of visitors it attracted. It also led to the establishment of the National Tidy Towns Competition, with most of the Tóstal committees around the country re-forming themselves into Tidy Towns Committees after the festival series ended.

The famous Great Southern red carpet made many an appearance during the Tóstal festivals. It was not laid when the World Ploughing Championships were held in Killarney in 1958, because most of the guests who packed the hotel on that occasion were arriving after a day in a very muddy field.

That was a year which would influence the lives of generations in Modern Ireland and one that had a tremendous influence on the future of the Great Southern Hotel.

But as the long queues of young men joined the trains at Killarney Station on their way to an emigrant's life, few would have guessed it.

Chapter 11

CHAPTER 11

Welcome to Modern Ireland

Ireland experienced an unprecedented transformation during the early sixties, which was brought about by a paper prepared by the secretary of the Department of Finance, T. K. Whitaker.

Published in 1956 it was called simply 'Economic Development'. The paper found an avid reader in Sean Lemass, then Minister for Industry and Commerce, who worked closely with Dr Whitaker to produce the ground-breaking 'Programme for Economic Development' in 1958 - a programme which was rapidly implemented after Lemass succeeded Eamon de Valera as Taoiseach in 1959.

The Programme for Economic Development was a blueprint for a New Ireland. Traditional conservative isolationism would be replaced by a new open economy in which overseas investment would be welcomed. New semi-state companies were established to promote exports and industry and Bord Fáilte was given a mandate and the money to step up the promotion of Ireland as a tourist destination and to develop the tourism product. It responded by taking initiatives in many areas of Irish life. It designed new signposts and co-operated with Local Authorities in a major re-signposting of the entire country. During the sixties the Board took a pro-active part in the creation of Festivals around the country including the Festival of Kerry, Galway Oyster Festival and the Wexford Opera Festival.

Access to Ireland was also improving. Back in the forties the first flying boats crossed the Atlantic and landed on the broad stretches of the Shannon Estuary, and a few years later the British Overseas Aircraft Corporation (BOAC) began regular scheduled flights from the USA to Foynes. The company next extended the service to land conventional aircraft at Rineanna and so Shannon Airport was born. During the fifties air travel into Shannnon and the Dublin airport at Collinstown grew steadily, but it was only in the early sixties that significant numbers of tourists began to arrive at Irish airports in the larger aircraft which were coming on stream. Killarney was a prime destination for these visitors, and the Great Southern Hotel buzzed with the sound of American accents.

The hotel was soon to have yet another new owner, albeit one closely related to CIE. Dr C. S. 'Todd' Andrews, who was appointed as full-time chairman of CIE in 1958 took the view that the hotels should be sold off to a new owner. In his autobiography he recalls that he recognised that the functional relationship between the railway and the hotels ceased once the bus and motor car replaced the railway for those whom the hotels were designed to serve.

'However they (the hotels) were still valuable assets....and we decided to enlarge and modernise them in order to cater for the increased traffic which the tourist industry was endeavouring to develop. For decoration purposes we were able to avail ourselves of the Arts Council scheme under which modern Irish paintings were supplied at a (fair) price for display in public buildings. The scheme gave a considerable boost to Irish artists and we were proud to be associated on a large scale with it.'

Welcoming An Taoiseach, Sean Lemass, to an IMI conference at the Great Southern Hotel Killarney were (from left) Ivor Kenny, director general IMI and Michael Rigby-Jones, president IMI (Head porter Denis Collins is in the background)

Many of the paintings acquired by CIE under that scheme still hang in the Great Southern Hotels in Killarney, Parknasilla and Galway.

In the early sixties, CIE also began an intensive promotion of Ireland in overseas markets. Its prime purpose was to attract visitors in groups who would travel by rail and coach, but it also worked in close association with its own Great Southern group and with other Irish hotels. Killarney was the principal destination for these groups outside of Dublin and the Great Southern Hotel played host to coach tour visitors who arrived daily. This business subsequently became the biggest retailer abroad of Irish holiday packages and it continues to thrive as CIE Tours International. Its marketing efforts in America were helped by a stream of positive publicity emanating from the visit to Ireland by President John F. Kennedy in 1963. Great Southern Hotel Killarney also provided its share of 'celebs' with Jackie Kennedy, Princess Grace of Monaco and Pat Nixon all staying there during the sixties.

In his book *On the Move*, which deals with the history of CIE, Micheál Ó Riain writes:

'Whether the existence of the hotels was a main catalyst for CIE's high profile in tourist development or whether the stimulus came from the natural role of a transport company in developing new traffic may be a matter for debate. CIE was proud of its hotels and they consistently returned a modest profit which, in view of their age and the location of some of them, was a creditable achievement. It is fair to say that outside of Dublin and Cork in the early sixties they were the only significant hotels in Ireland which were being adequately modernised and promoted.'

Liam Ryan who implemented a major investment programme when he was general manager of the Great Southern Hotel Killarney

Todd Andrews nevertheless was anxious to operate the hotels at arms length and in 1961 CIE transferred their ownership to a new subsidiary company called Ostlanna Iompair Eireann (Irish Transport Hotels). In that same year of 1961 Liam Ryan became general manager of the Great Southern Hotel Killarney, and began to implement the investment programme planned by OIE. The main kitchen was modernised with the installation of cold rooms and new refrigeration equipment, a cocktail bar was created and a programme of upgrading bedrooms by installing en suite bathrooms was undertaken. This programme, which continued throughout the sixties, resulted in a slight reduction in the number of bedrooms at the hotel because frequently it was necessary to combine three rooms into two in order to accommodate the new ensuite bathrooms.

Long before the concept of 'organic food' became popular, Great Southern Hotel Killarney was able to source supplies of organically produced foods from its very own farm. The farm, located just behind the hotel was stocked with six cows, ten pigs (who dined on swill from the hotel) and 80 hens which combined to produce milk, eggs and bacon for the hotel kitchen. Large glass houses were used to produce early vegetables, fruit and tomatoes and the farm manager took pride in delivering rhubarb to the hotel kitchen on St Stephen's Day. Farm and hotel staff joined in celebration in 1967 when a two-year-old heifer bred on the farm won the title of 'Best Pure Bred Kerry Heifer' at the Kerry Agricultural Show.

The fresh produce from the farm was given the benefit of a culinary style which combined the traditions of Escoffier with the concept of 'home cooking'. Roasts were carved in the kitchen to order, chickens were cooked in the enormous ovens and fresh fish was turned on the pan. Fresh vegetables and of course Kerry potatoes were in plentiful supply and helpings were large.

Among those to savour these culinary delights, which also included a 'Full Irish' breakfast, were hundreds of Civil Servants who had enrolled in the Institute of Public Administration which was founded by Dr Tom Barrington in 1957. A Kerryman, Dr Barrington had a great love for his native country, and his book *Discovering Kerry* remains one of the most informative guides to 'The Kingdom'. The IPA was established to provide public servants with academic qualifications and Tom Barrington promoted the idea of a Public Administration College which would be located in Muckross House. While the plan did not come to fruition, the IPA held some of its early courses in Killarney with the participants staying at the Great Southern Hotel. Ten residential courses, each of five weeks' duration were held between 1961 and 1964, attended by assistant departmental secretaries, principal officers, local government and state company managers. Sean Lemass officially launched the courses which were supported by the United Nations and the lecturers included a senior professor from Columbia University. As the courses were usually held in Spring, the IPA produced valuable off-peak business for Great Southern. They ceased after the Dublin-based School of Public Administration was established by the IPA in 1964.

Arriving at the conference centre of the Great Southern Hotel are (from left) Mrs Máirín Lynch, head porter Denis Collins, assistant head porter P.J. Harnett, An Taoiseach Jack Lynch, chief executive of Great Southern Hotels, John Byrne, and general manager Great Southern Hotel Killarney, Louis O'Hara

Following hard on the heels of the Civil Servants were some very well-heeled businessmen who flocked to Killarney in the Spring to attend the National Conference of the Irish Management Institute. The IMI was established in 1952 to enhance the expertise of Irish business managers through educational courses, communications and its National Conference. The Great Southern Hotel Killarney was chosen as the venue for the conference from an early stage, but initially the business sessions were held in Árus Phádraig, a community hall owned by the Franciscan Fathers and located in the grounds of the Friary.

Richard Whelan recalls porters from the hotel ferrying hundreds of chairs across the road to the hall in preparation for the conference as well as crockery and boilers for the coffee breaks. The businessmen (and they were virtually all men) stayed at the Great Southern where the formal banquet was held, and in other hotels in the town. As the conference grew in size and stature from 150 to 650 participants, it became clear that Árus Phádraig was not a suitable venue for the meetings and this prompted the Board of Great Southern Hotels to develop a purpose-built conference centre in the grounds, the first of its kind outside of Dublin. The conference centre was opened in 1968 by Jack Lynch who was then Minister for Industry and Commerce, together with a new wing which added 36 en-suite bedrooms to the hotel.

The relationship between the Irish Management Institute, Killarney and the Great Southern Hotel has blossomed over the years. During the heyday of the IMI from the mid-sixties to the mid-seventies, many of the world's outstanding business gurus spoke at the conference including Paul Drucker and Tom Peters who joined leading Irish businessmen like Tony O'Reilly, Michael Smurfit, Todd Andrews and Kerry's own Denis Brosnan.

A special Conference Train brought delegates from Dublin under the full glare of the media. Telefís Eireann, which had recently come on air, gave the event saturation coverage, showing the country's business leaders taking lunch on the train, sipping coffee on the Great Southern Hotel lawns or providing sound bites for business journalists. The highlight of each annual conference was an address by the Taoiseach on the final Saturday morning and among those to fulfil this engagement were Sean Lemass, Jack Lynch, Liam Cosgrave, Charles Haughey, Dr Garrett Fitzgerald, Albert Reynolds, John Bruton and, most recently, Bertie Ahern.

The new conference centre could not exist on one annual event, however, nor did it have to. From its earliest days the Great Southern was a popular conference venue, playing host to many annual gatherings of professional bodies, companies like Guinness and Irish Dunlop and, of course, the trade unions.

The Great Southern Killarney has been a trade union hotel since the mid-1950s when hotel workers in the town were organised by John Carroll, who was later to become president of the Irish Transport and General Workers Union (now SIPTU). He established the first Union group in the hotel which elected porter Louis Berger, a former studio photographer, as its shop steward. The hotel remains organised today with staff represented by both SIPTU and the Transport Salaried Staff Association (TSSA). A new partnership agreement was concluded in 2001 which modernised working arrangements and the pay structure at all Great Southern hotels.

A welcome for Taoiseach Charles J. Haughey when he visited the hotel

Taoiseach Liam Cosgrave addresses the IMI Conference at the Great Southern Hotel, Killarney

Head porter Mossie Horgan joined the hotel as a page boy in 1961 spending his days operating the lift, bringing messages to guests, polishing brass stair rods and other duties. He has fond memories of two outstanding women who were then part of the management staff, Vera Chapman and Sheila Harte. Known to staff as 'Reverend Mother' and to guests and friends as 'Chappie', Vera Chapman came to Killarney as an assistant manager and remained with the hotel in various management capacities until her death in 2001. 'She could spot a fleck of dust a mile away', Mossie Horgan recalls. 'Under her watchful eye the hotel was a model of cleanliness and hygiene.' Sheila Harte who was executive housekeeper and later accommodation services manager at the hotel was previously general manager at the Great Southern Hotel, Kenmare. A true professional, she was a founder member of the Association of Hotel Accommodation Management which is now the Irish Accommodation Services Institute. An annual award presented by IASI was created in her honour.

Killarney shared the prosperity which was enjoyed by the Irish people through much of the sixties and was a particular beneficiary of the boom in tourism. The Great Southern was buzzing with coach tour groups and a new phenomenon called the 'incentive tour'. These were usually employees of American companies who were brought to Killarney as a sort of bonus for achieving sales or production targets. The companies had large budgets and made sure that their employees got 'only the best'. Niall Kenny, who was then general manager of The Great Southern Hotel, responded by providing special meals, including an Irish bacon and cabbage menu and a cabaret show featuring Chris Curran, tenor Louis Browne and Bill McMahon.

Even greater numbers of tourists were promised by a new phenomenon - the car ferry. Until the end of the fifties the task of bringing a private motor car to Ireland from Britain or Europe was, to say the least, onerous. Cars had to be lifted into the holds of cargo ships by crane and removed by a similar method when they reached their destination. And if that was not enough, highly restrictive rules governed the driving of 'foreign registered motor vehicles' in the Republic. Much of this red tape was eliminated in the more liberal trade regime of the sixties and motorists were given a further incentive to bring their cars to Ireland with the advent

An Taoiseach Bertie Ahern relaxing at the Great Southern Hotel Killarney

of new roll-on-roll-off ferries. While it was the early seventies before a proper service linked Ireland directly with Europe, the Irish sea ferry routes were planned in the mid-sixties with the promise of bringing large numbers of British motorists to Ireland. Dermot Ryan, an innovative entrepreneur and hotelier, responded to the development by building a number of budget hotels and he was followed quickly by Great Southern Hotels which built its first 'motor inns' at Rosslare and Killarney. The Torc Great Southern in Killarney, which opened in 1969, was not a 'motel' in the American sense, but it did provide budget accommodation for motorists and a limited service - something along the lines of the 'New Hotel' which had been demolished in 1923. Before this CIE had itself encouraged the provision of tourist accommodation including a number of railway carriages which were parked near the Garden Cottage (the former Refreshment Rooms) and used as holiday homes. The new 'motor hotels' were designed 'in-house' at Great Southern Hotels' head offices by a team of architects headed by Paddy O'Shea. The team had a staff of 14 people in the late sixties, all busily engaged in construction, renovation and refurbishment projects at the group's hotels.

Like the entire population of Ireland, they were optimistic about the future of the country, the economy, the tourist industry and specifically Great Southern Hotels.

They could not have foreseen what was about to happen north of the Border.

Chapter 12

CHAPTER 12

Surviving The 'Troubles'

Early in 1969 a march by members of 'People's Democracy', a civil rights organisation, was ambushed by Loyalists at Burntollet, Co. Derry as it made its way from Belfast to Derry City. More than 300 people were injured and what became known as the 'Troubles' had begun.

For the next thirty years, until the Good Friday Agreement of 1998, Northern Ireland would be torn apart by bombs, gunfire and rioting and the entire island and its people would suffer deeply.

Initially however life at the Great Southern Hotel Killarney continued normally and in the early years of the Troubles business held up fairly well. Eamonn McKeon, now chief executive of Great Southern Hotels, joined the company in 1969 and recalls that work on upgrading the Great Southern Killarney continued, with the removal of fireplaces from bedrooms and the installation of new bathrooms. Indeed by 1971 every room at the hotel was an *en-suite*.

Christmas too remained a special time with a huge tree erected in the lounge, music provided by Bob Roberts trio, gifts for all the guests, special menus in the restaurant and every detail overseen by the eagle-eyed Vera Chapman.

The tourism season then was short. Even in Killarney there was not a lot of business before Whit Sunday and after the end of September. During the winter months therefore some hotels closed while those that remained open looked around for whatever business was available. One of the 'catches' prized by Killarney hoteliers was 'The Bar', the travelling group of solicitors, barristers, judges and their assorted staffs who descended upon Killarney for sittings of the Munster Circuit. For many years The Bar had its headquarters at the Great Southern Hotel, but at one stage its august members were 'edged out' early in the year to make way for an unexpected influx of tourists. They packed up their wigs and headed 'en masse' for the International Hotel - and it took some of the best legal minds in the country and the charismatic presence of 'Chappie' to get them back.

Back however they eventually came, with their own pieces of antique silver which were used at the 'Mess', the formal lawyers' dinners. One particularly valuable claret jug 'went missing' during a particularly long and perhaps less formal evening, precipitating a massive investigation among the hotel staff. It was subsequently found under a chair where it had been cunningly concealed by a rotund advocate whose interest lay more in its content than in its intrinsic value.

Among the lawyers who lived 'for many a Winter' at the Great Southern was the now-retired High Court Judge Dermot Kinlen, who recalls that the hotel would remain open to 'some special guests', even at times when it was officially closed. 'When I first stayed in the late fifties we were given an all inclusive rate of sixteen shillings (one euro) per day for bed, breakfast, lunch and dinner, which could only be changed by giving us six month's notice. It remained constant for some time, but then we got notice that it was going up to eighteen shillings, then twenty-one shillings and finally, I think, twenty-six shillings.'

The lawyers nevertheless remained loyal to the hotel and none more so than Dermot Kinlen who almost became a member of the staff. Each year at Christmas he took on the role of 'Santa Claus', a tradition which happily continues, although temporarily suspended in 2001 when the hotel was closed for redevelopment.

Dermot was also producer of the Great Southern Hotels 'Tops of the Town' shows in the sixties and seventies. These productions brought the entire staff together in a great team effort and are fondly remembered by Paddy Ryan, Mossy Horgan, P. J. Hartnett, Tommy Regan and other 'Great Southern' stalwarts. Teresa Keogh recalls that the shows were of a very high standard, with professional entertainer Paschal Spelman travelling down from Galway to direct several productions. Jimmy Cullinane was the Master of Ceremonies and the shows included spectacular scenes from Broadway musicals such as *Oklahoma* and *The Sound of Music*.

Duchess of York, Sarah Ferguson, pictured during a visit to Killarney with former General Manager Eamon Daly

Great Southern reached the national final of the competition on one occasion and the entire cast and supporters travelled by special train to Dublin and then by coach to the Gaiety Theatre for the event.

The hotel became even more closely involved in show business during the mid-seventies when David Lean came to Kerry to make his film *Ryan's Daughter*. Most of the film was shot on the Dingle Peninsula where Lean had an Irish village built as a set. His headquarters were in the Great Southern Hotel Killarney where the film company booked out two complete floors for a two-year period. The restaurant was converted into a cinema with its own tip-up seats and silver screen. It was here that David Lean and his team would gather every evening to view the 'rushes' of the day's shoot, deciding what they could use and what needed to be shot again. And much indeed had to be re-shot, as scene after scene failed to satisfy the director, who was one of the film industry's most notorious perfectionists. Locals recall one scene which was shot on a strand near Dingle and involved a confrontation between two of the film's actors, Robert Mitchum and Trevor Howard. The crew had spent several days setting up the scene, with cameras on cranes and trolleys and a myriad of lighting. Then they waited for the perfect weather, which eventually arrived, and the scene was shot, again and again and again. Looking at the rushes that evening David Lean is reported to have been very happy initially, but suddenly he jumped up from his chair exclaiming. 'It will not do - there are no seagulls'.

He would not settle for the scene and instead had it all set up again, waited for a repeat of the precise weather he wanted and had the scene re-shot. This time, however, the seagull problem was solved by a man with a bucket of fish who dropped them into the waves at the end of the beach just before each shoot, thereby guaranteeing the immediate arrival of a flock of birds.

At least until near the end of the day when the seagulls were so full of fish they did not bother to respond to the bucket of mackerel.

During the making of *Ryan's Daughter*, the Great Southern was an ideal location for celebrity-spotting with stars like John Mills, Sarah Miles, Robert Mitchum, Trevor Howard, the writer Robert Bolt and Irish actors like Marie Keane and Des Keogh in regular attendance - and of course the great David Lean and his 'companion,' 'Miss Hodgekiss,' residing in the Presidential Suite. They were all looked after with great care and professionalism by the hotel staff under their own 'director' - general manager Niall Kenny.

They were not the only celebrities visiting the hotel, however. The President of Ireland Eamon de Valera stayed in Room 46 whenever he came to Killarney and a special bed, whose iron headboard was inlaid with mother of pearl, was reserved for him. Mossie Horgan recalls that the bed broke shortly before one Presidential visit and was repaired just in time by a local blacksmith.

Dev was not always happy with his special bed and said as much one sunny morning to the hall porter. The conversation, which was conducted through the medium of Irish, ran:

Jackie O'Sullivan, former head barman and a Killarney employee for 44 years, presently a Director of Great Southern Hotels

Dev: 'Tá an leaba seo go h-ana cruaidh. Ni raibh aon chodladh agam.'

Porter: 'Inseoidh mé sin do Bean a Tí, Miss Chapman.'

Dev: 'Go raibh maith agat agus go n-eirí an bóthar leat.'

Told about the incident during the days of President de Valera's state funeral a young trainee manager is reported to have said:

'Sure if he slept in that bed - no wonder the man is dead.'

When the *Ryan's Daughter* crew moved from Kerry to complete the film, Great Southern Hotel was once again able to reclaim its Malton Room restaurant - the temporary cinema. The 'Malton Room' opened in 1971 and was modelled on grill bars like the 'Claddagh' at the Great Southern Hotel Galway, the 'Saddle Room' at the Shelbourne in Dublin and the 'Bianconi Grill' at the Royal Hibernian Hotel on Dawson Street, Dublin.

The walls of the Malton Room were hung with a complete set of Malton Prints depicting 18th Century Dublin buildings and streetscapes which remain in the hotel, this time in a new 'Malton Room' designed for meetings.

The service included an element of 'theatre' with waiters preparing dishes at the table including flambes, 'steak tartare', fondues and 'crêpes suzette'. The menu was designed by head chef Franz Knoblauch, who later established a successful restaurant in Killarney and the head waiter was Wim Mickles. Food fashions change however and in the eighties the style of the Malton Room menu changed to French with an emphasis on 'haute cuisine'. The restaurant was closed in 1991, but has now become 'Peppers' a new speciality restaurant which features Mediterranean and 'New Irish' cuisine and is again distinguished by the collection of modern Irish paintings which hang on its walls.

Micheal Rosney, pictured at the Great Southern Hotel Killarney where he was general manager with his uncle Joe Lucey, also a former general manager of the hotel

Visitors to the Great Southern Hotel over the years invariably remember the warmth of the welcome they receive, the open fire in the lobby and the friendly professional service in the restaurants and bars. These unique experiences are the result of a long tradition of professionalism and dedication by the entire staff of the hotel including those who are most 'visible' to guests - the hall porters, receptionists, dining room, restaurant and bar staff. The hotel has produced its share of 'legends' over the years, including Jimmy Cullinane, Denis Collins, P. J. Hartnett, Jackie O'Sullivan and the incumbent hall porter, Mossie Horgan.

Many also remember the immaculately maintained, gardens which were tended by a team which included Paddy Ryan and who were winners in the Bord Fáilte 'Hotel Gardens Competition' on many occasions. Denis Collins was known and photographed by thousands and thousands of coach visitors to the Great Southern. He invariably boarded the coach on its arrival to greet visitors with a 'Céad Míle Fáilte' and over his 40 years at the Hall Porter's desk he is reputed to have issued more than a million admonitions to guests to remember to leave their room keys.

Jimmy Cullinane, a Dubliner, who worked on the railway dining cars before joining 'Great Southern,' is remembered as a great professional head waiter, a charming host and a true gentleman. Keenly interested in a wide range of activities, he was involved in many community activities and turned his pen to the occasional piece of poetry.

One of Jimmy's poems was composed to mark the Golden Jubilee of Killarney Races and was published in the book *Horse Racing* by Killarney author Finbarr Slattery. It opens:

This is our Golden Jubilee Year
We mean to celebrate
It's a milestone in our history
So hurry - don't be late
We're going to do it justice
And drink a special toast
There is a lot to tell you
We're not afraid to boast.

Four stanzas later, the Races have been eulogised and the poem concludes:

Today we have a lovely track
The most scenic in the land
Excellent catering facilities
Enjoymentwise, it's grand
We're a nation of Saints and Sinners
And like the races best
Finbarr (Slattery) will give you some winners
And I will give you the rest.

Killarney races of course filled the Great Southern and other hotels whenever they were held, but a more regular brigade of sports people were the golfers who flocked to Killarney over the years. They included Herbert Warren Wind, a distinguished American golf writer who wrote enthusiastically about the Killarney course in a book which he published following a tour of Irish golf course in 1967. It was this book called *The Greens of Ireland* and related articles which first alerted American golfers to the magnificent links courses at Ballybunion, Lahinch and Portmarnock and which helped put Irish golf on the world map. Herbert Wind played the Killarney course with Captain D. Connell, the club secretary, and later dined at the Great Southern with Finbarr Slattery, Ivo O'Sullivan (the club captain), Captain O'Connell, and Dr Billy O'Sullivan.

'We talked nothing but golf for five straight hours', he later wrote. 'I heard more original thinking about the game that evening than I had for years.'

He goes on to describe the origins of golf in Killarney, as told to him by Finbarr Slattery:

'Golf first took root in Killarney in 1891, the same year it was brought to Lahinch. That summer, nine holes were laid out in the town deer park. Willie Park Jr, one of the top Scottish professionals and golf architects, designed the bunkering. In time, the course was extended to eighteen holes, but there was never much golf fever in Killarney, despite the game's inexpensiveness. As late as 1916 annual dues for the members was onlv a touch over six dollars. The man who changed all this was the late Viscount Castlerosse, in his last years the sixth Earl of Kenmare. A large, ponderous man, Castlerosse became a well-known personality in Britain during the 1930s as the gossip columnist of the London *Sunday Express*. He was, in fact, the first of that breed in Fleet Street, and so good at the job that he was accorded a full page. As a young man Castlerosse had been a skillful enough golfer to make his University team. As his girth increased, so did his handicap. but he continued to play a more than respectable game and, if anything, his enthusiasm for golf became more and more intense. In the late 1930s, after he had come into the family property fronting on Lough Leane, the largest of the four lakes in Killarney, he was in a position to fulfill a long-nourished dream to build a championship-calibre golf course. First, a corporation was set up, part of the shares going to Killarney hoteliers, who contributed capital, and the other part going to Castlerosse who contributed the land. Then Castlerosse lined up the golf architect he wanted, Sir Guy Campbell, an experienced designer whose many credits included brilliant revisions of the old links at Rye and Deal, in south-eastern England. In Sir Guy's opinion, the configuration of the land at Killarney was ideal, and en route to mapping out a preliminary layout he walked his acres tirelessly and tossed around his ideas at regular intervals with Castlerosse and Henry Longhurst, the gifted English golf journalist, who was one of Castlerosse's closest Fleet Street friends. The three were in agreement that the course they were after should have the same close-knit turfy grass that makes seaside links such a delight but that, at the same time, it should have the basic flavour of a lakeside course and take full advantage of the scenic glory of Lough Leane and Macgillycuddy's Reeks, the rugged mountains that rise just to the west of the lakes. During the Second World War, Castlerosse personally altered some features of the holes that Campbell devised and, as a final touch, landscaped many of the green areas with masses of hydrangeas, rhododendrons, azaleas, laburnum and other flowering shrubs and trees. When the course was ultimately opened for play after the war, Castlerosse confidently expected it to, be 'successful'. He saw the course as 'the beginning of a new movement which will make the south of Ireland, and Kerry in particular, the playground par excellence of two continents.'

Killarney Golf Club

And he was indeed prophetic. The course has since been expanded many times, and a second championship course has been added. Killarney is now among the most popular golf venues in Ireland, hosting many major championships and attracting thousands of golfers to the Great Southern and other hotels.

Well into the seventies visitors to the Great Southern could see a line of jarvey cars parked on the road outside the hotel. The Killarney jarveys up to then dressed formally in swallow tailed coats and bowler hats and complemented the top hatted hall porters in their dark blue uniforms. They had a good working relationship with the hotel and there was widespread mourning when one of their number, Michael Murphy, was killed by a rearing horse.

Once a year, however, access to both the hotel and the railway station became a little more difficult. The road from the perimeter of the hotel to the railway remained the private property of Great Southern Hotels and, in order to protect this right, hall porters from the hotel sealed off the road for one day in July each year, formally giving permission to train travellers and hotel guests to pass through.

That same road proved its value in 1971 when a fire broke out at the hotel during the night. It was spotted by Garda Sgt John Leen who alerted the fire brigade and the hotel manager David Byrne. His prompt action probably saved the entire building.

During the traumatic seventies, Killarney remained peaceful apart from an isolated incident in 1976 when a small 'device' was discovered in the Torc Great Southern Hotel. Events in the North were, however, to have a dramatic influence on the hotel's owners, Ostlanna Iompair Eirann. The company was in expansionist mood in the late sixties, opening its brand new motor hotels at Rosslare and Killarney and a gourmet fish restaurant called Restaurant na Mara at Dún Laoghaire. It was unsuccessful in finding a suitable site for a Dublin hotel and looked instead to Belfast where it bought the Russell Court Hotel close to the city centre. The existing building was demolished and replaced by a modern 200 bedroom hotel. The new Russell Court Hotel opened on 11th August 1972, but suffered extensive damage when it was bombed on 25th September and had to close immediately. A claim for compensation to Belfast Corporation was successful and the hotel was repaired and 70 bedrooms were re-opened in May 1973. After a difficult period of trading, a second bomb exploded in the hotel on St Patrick's Day 1975 and as a result the hotel closed permanently.

The losses associated with the short life of the Russell Court Hotel had a major adverse impact on the finances of OIE. They came at a time when tourism in the Republic of Ireland declined sharply as a result of the publicity associated with the Troubles in Northern Ireland and an international oil crisis which produced petrol shortages and major price increases. This in turn sparked off a rapid rise in Irish inflation which in turn led to a lack of competitiveness as a holiday destination. As a major player in the tourism industry, Great Southern Hotels found itself exposed to an extremely difficult market and, like many other hotels in the country, incurred financial losses.

CIE commissioned the international consultants Arthur D. Little to report on the situation and they recommended an immediate equity investment of £1.5m. The Board considered this report and decided that CIE would increase its equity holding in OIE and would convert an existing loan of £440,000 into equity capital. The resort hotels at Bundoran, Sligo, Mulrany and Kenmare (but not Parknasilla) were sold as were all surplus lands around the hotels. The Russell Court would remain closed and would be sold.

By 1978 CIE was optimistic enough to report that the 'strategy adopted in 1976 to sell four hotels and to reinvest the proceeds in refurbishing the remaining six hotels has been successful. The outlook for 1978 is for a significant increase in profits.'

During these difficult times Great Southern Hotel, Killarney continued to maintain an exceptionally high standard of service under the guidance of a succession of distinguished general managers including Louis O'Hara, Niall Kenny, Tim Corcoran, Denis Hurley and Brendan Maher.

But the days of the link between Great Southern Hotels and the railways were numbered. By 1984 the accumulated losses of OIE reached £9.85m and the Government decided to transfer their ownership to the state tourism training agency CERT. Note 6 of the accounts of CIE for 1984 records the transfer with brevity:

'The share capital held by Córas Iompair Eireann in the subsidiary company Ostlanna Iompair Eireann Teoranta was disposed on 9th March 1984 for £1.'

CERT may have acquired Great Southern Hotels for one pound, but the Board of GSH was soon required to commission a number of refurbishment projects, the biggest of which was the provision of a new roof for the Great Southern Hotel, Killarney in 1985.

The hotels remained in the ownership of CERT for six years until they were sold again in 1990 for £10m (€12.7m), this time to the present owners, Aer Rianta, which was to develop the group through expansion and renewal in the era of the 'Celtic Tiger.'

Chapter 13

CHAPTER 13

New Life for an Old Lady

Somewhere in Ireland around the end of the eighties, a tiger cub was born. It was not in a zoo or a circus, because this was a different sort of cat, an economic one which would become known around the world as 'The Celtic Tiger'.

The name was borrowed from the 'Asian Tiger' economies of the Far East which blossomed in the eighties and it has the same resonance. Economic policies followed by a succession of Irish Governments combined with a favourable international economic climate to bring about a transformation within the country. Unemployment and involuntary emigration, which had been a feature of the economy since the foundation of the State, all but disappeared, taxes were substantially reduced and low interest rates encouraged investment.

Tourism was a key driver in this remarkable economic turnaround. The size of the industry had doubled in the eighties and doubled again in the nineties to a point where tourism earnings topped the £3bn mark and visitor numbers exceeded three million towards the end of the nineties.

Hotels shared in this prosperity with more than 100 new properties opening between 1993 and 1998. The new hotels were located throughout the country, but the biggest concentrations were in Dublin and the principal resorts. Great Southern Hotels itself built new hotels at Dublin and Cork airports. Only one hotel opened in Killarney between 1933 and 1959, but up to a dozen, including a number of four-star properties, were built in and around the town during the 1990s.

With new confidence in the future of tourism, Killarney hoteliers and other tourism interests organised a number of successful marketing initiatives including the 'Roaring Twenties Festival' which ran for five years. This event, held over the St Patrick's weekend, provided an opportunity for local people and visitors to re-live the Jazz Age. Vintage car parades, fancy dress balls, an international Barber Shop Quartet competition and casino nights were all part of the fun. Great Southern Hotel was the venue for the major events of the festival and its unique style and atmosphere contributed to its authenticity.

Visitor and commercial business was buoyant during these years with many incentive groups and coach tours filling the hotel. General managers Michael Rosney, Matt Sherlock and Eamon Daly enjoyed running a hotel which was thriving. Several investment projects were undertaken including a conservatory-style bar which was added in 1991 and the renovation of bedrooms in 1993.

Despite regular investment however the 'Grand Old Lady of Killarney' was showing her age. Renovations over the years had created new facilities and maintained the visual appearance of the hotel, but serious problems had developed behind the plastered walls and in the 'engine room' of the building.

The restored Garden Room (Don Mac Monagle)

The elegance of the refurbished lounge (Don Mac Monagle)

Conor Hennigan, general manager, Great Southern Hotel, Killarney

Luxury in a Great Southern Hotel Killarney guest room (Don Mac Monagle)

19th century elegance and 21st century amenities at the Great Southern Hotel Killarney
(Don Mac Monagle)

Eamonn McKeon, chief executive of Great Southern Hotels, had been aware of the decline in the structure for some time. 'The point was reached where we had to arrest the deterioration of the fabric of the building in order to guarantee the future of the hotel into the next century', he says.

That decision was taken by the Directors in the mid-nineties, with the full backing of the Board of Aer Rianta.

A €14m plan (more than 600 times the original cost of the hotel), was devised to return the Great Southern Hotel to its former glory by restoring the building, upgrading it to the most exacting specifications and re-creating, in a modern context, the Victorian character which had been its claim to fame for almost 150 years.

This time the commission went to architects Traynor O'Toole and it fell to Deirdre Parkinson to preserve Frederick Darley's building for future generations.

Eamon McKeon, chief executive, Great Southern Hotels

Before work could commence, however, it was necessary to critically examine the building to assess its architectural heritage. Conservationist Garry Miley was commissioned to prepare a 'Conservation Report' which listed the architectural aspects of the hotel which should be preserved, and this formed part of the planning process.

The final plan involved a large amount of work designed to preserve the building, to enable it to comply with modern standards of safety and efficiency. The entire building would be re-wired, large areas of plumbing would be renewed, items such as a 40-year-old boiler would be replaced, state of the art telecommunications facilities would be incorporated and fire and noise insulation would be upgraded.

It was decided to create a number of new, larger bedrooms by knocking three rooms into two and this enabled the architects to provide facilities such as dressing rooms, large bathrooms and stand-alone shower units. In addition sixteen new guestrooms were added and 100 rooms of the hotel were refurbished.

While the new and refurbished guestrooms are now equipped with safety and security features, computer modem points, inter-active digital television and a host of other amenities, their Victorian elegance has also been preserved through specially designed bed throws, velvet and silk drapes and carefully chosen art. The new rooms are, however, an exception as they have modern décor with bright bold colours in a design which has proven to be very successful at the Great Southern Hotel in Cork. With the construction of new rooms and the demolition of others, the hotel now has 172 guest rooms of international five-star standard.

Final plans for the project were completed late in 2000 and planning permission was granted in June 2001. Following a tender process the contract was awarded to John F. Supple and Co. of Cork, which is listed on the Register of Heritage Contractors of the Construction Industry Federation. The Great Southern closed its doors early in September 2001 and the builders went on site immediately.

Early on in the construction, dry rot was discovered in the interior of the building. This came as little surprise, because water was seeping into the hotel prior to the replacement of the roof in 1985 and the damage had been done then. The discovery meant that large sections of walls and ceilings had to be removed, the rotted timbers removed and replaced with either new timber or metal. After removing floors and ceilings the builders also discovered that dried leaves and turf dust had been used extensively in the original construction as an insulation material. 'It seems to have been very effective', says Deirdre Parkinson.

The conservatory bar was removed as part of the project and replaced with a block wall which now encloses the newly designed bar. Partitions were removed from some guest rooms and a number of fireplaces, which had been plastered over, were revealed. It was decided to preserve one of these bedroom fireplaces as a link to the Victorian origins of the building.

The first element of the restored hotel to be seen by the visitor is the handsome portico. This leads to a new front door, which mirrors the original hall door of the building, and replaces the revolving door which had been in place for several decades. Behind this, the fireplace with its blazing coal fire, which has been a welcoming feature of the hotel since its inception, has been retained and the floor of the entrance hall has now been laid with Spanish marble.

This area is now separated from the 'Reception Salon' (originally the Coffee Room) by a timber and glass screen modelled on a similar screen which was placed here when the hotel was first built. This splendid space has now been completely refurbished, with a new stained glass skylight admitting floods of natural light, while hand-made carpets by McMurray's of Galway and furnishings, including some of the most comfortable armchairs in the land, reflect the Victorian era. Crystal chandeliers from Waterford Glass hang from the high ceiling while palms and exotic plants are placed around the floor. Three lounges (formerly a writing room, smoking room and needlework room) surround the salon. The larger of these lounges was also used for many years as a souvenir shop and part of it was a manager's office. A safe used by the managers was discovered hidden behind a shutter, and retained.

The magnificent Garden Room at the Great Southern Hotel impressed visitors and writers from the beginning and it is now charming a new generation. The arched ceiling, with its ornate plasterwork now radiates white and gold, while the huge bay window looks out on the hotel gardens. Irish handmade carpet is on the floor, and the dining chairs, by Extreme Lifestyles of Kilcullen, are a combination of Italian woodwork and Irish upholstery.

Guests can choose to dine here or in 'Peppers', the hotel's contemporary restaurant which features modern Irish cuisine and is home to a collection of paintings by contemporary Irish artists. 'Peppers' is located in the former 'Malton Room' and that title, as we have already mentioned, together with the collection of Malton prints, has now been given to one of a series of new meeting rooms in the hotel, which are fitted with modern AV and communications equipment.

The Punchbowl bar has been remodelled to create a 'club' atmosphere with its hardwood bar counter, Victorian wood panelling and Georgian fireplace. It takes its name from a painting of the Punchbowl Mountain which hangs over the fireplace.

Not all the developments at the Great Southern, Killarney are visible to the guest. Meals are now prepared in a new state of the art kitchen on two levels fitted with the most modern catering equipment, and complies with HACCP hygiene regulations.

The final element in the revitalisation of the hotel has been a major expansion and development of the Conference and Leisure Centre. The architects have made extensive use of natural wood in the frontage of the expanded Centre , which now has resonances of an ancient Irish Ring Fort. The Muckross Suite can

The foyer of the new Conference Centre at the Great Southern Hotel, Killarney

Relaxing in the Leisure Centre at the Great Southern Hotel, Killarney

Staff of the Great Southern Hotel Killarney

accommodate up to 850 people for a meeting or banquet and comes complete with an enlarged stage area with its own AV and lighting systems, a new large bar, a spacious exhibition hall and a break-out area which leads directly to the gardens. The Mangerton Suite has also been remodelled and is now a tiered theatre with its own facilities. Both suites are serviced by a new kitchen.

And for those who want to relax during conference breaks or during their hotel stay, the swimming pool at the Leisure Centre has been upgraded and special treatment rooms offering aromatherapy, reflexology and ki-massage have been added.

All of these new facilities were admired by Minister Mary O'Rourke in her final week in office, when she officially reopened the Great Southern Hotel, Killarney in June 2002. She was joined in her admiration of the revitalised hotel by 150 guests, by general manager Conor Hennigan and by the entire staff of the hotel, many of whom have seen its colourful history unfold.

To them, and to their guests, the Great Southern is something special - a place of relaxation, comfort and fine food, where the 'Céad Míle Fáilte' never ceases. A place which has been 'home' to Victorians, to royalty, to soldiers and their prisoners, to film directors and actors, to sports stars and their followers, to poets, politicians, and captains of industry - but mostly to visitors who have flocked to Killarney for almost two centuries, to spend a time in 'Heaven's Reflex'.

It is the 'Grand Old Lady of Killarney' whose life, well into the future, is now assured.

Chapter 14

art

Great Southern Hotels has been a supporter of Irish artists since the 1960s and its collection of Irish paintings, which are displayed throughout its hotels, is much admired by guests from all over the world.

The paintings reproduced on the following pages are taken from the extensive collection displayed at the Great Southern Hotel Killarney.

Daffodils *by Helena Branicardi*

Another Bottle *by George Dunne*

Sybil Head *by Tom Greaney*

A Pint and a Read by Ted Jones

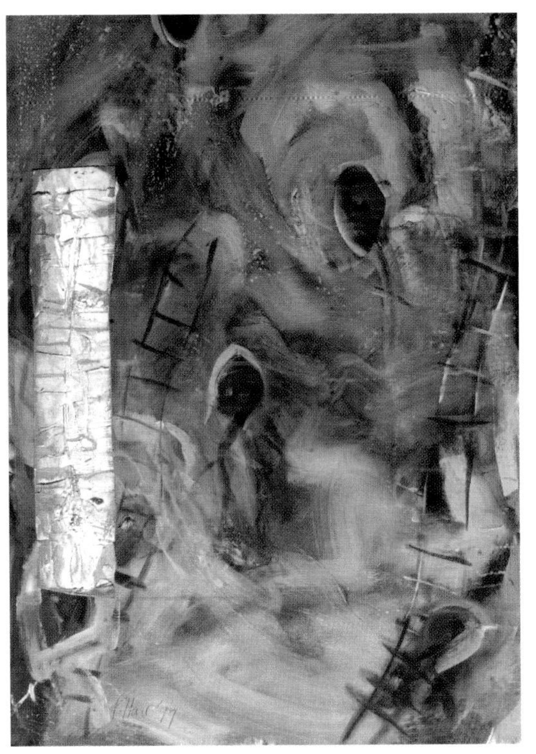

Winter Cherries by Patricia Hurl

Cleggan Cottages
by Rooney

Turf Saving
by Jim Huston

Swans
by Carl Batternay

John B. Keane
by John Shortt

Slea Head
by John Dinan

Hooked on the Laune
by Michael McCarthy

Harvest Pattern
by Ann Tallentine

Ladies View
by Fred Gruizinga

A Fine Pair
by Alex McKenna

The Punchbowl
by Sean O'Connor

The Long Acre
by Liam Jones

Wind
by Donald Teskey

Sunset on the Lakes
by Liam Jones

Western Sunset
by W. H. Burns

Index

Index